GOOD OLD-FASHIONED
TEATIME
TREATS

GOOD OLD-FASHIONED
TEATIME
TREATS

Jane Pettigrew

National Trust

First published in the United Kingdom in 2010 by
National Trust Books
10 Southcombe Street
London
W14 0RA

An imprint of Anova Books Company Ltd

ISBN: 9781905400904

A CIP catalogue record for this book is available from the British Library.

18 17 16 15 14 13 12 10
10 9 8 7 6 5 4 3 2 1

Reproduction by Dot Gradations Ltd, UK
Printed by Toppan Leefung Printing Ltd, China

This book can be ordered direct from the publisher at the website www.anovabooks.com,
or try your local bookshop. Also available at National Trust shops and www.nationaltrustbooks.co.uk.

CONTENTS

INTRODUCTION

In the early days of the National Trust, visitors to the properties were sometimes offered a cup of tea and a bun at the kitchen door or in some suitable corner of the house or garden. Nowadays, many properties provide morning coffee, lunches, afternoon teas and, sometimes, evening meals or special functions in prestigious and stylish restaurants. The food is always of a high standard, and in many areas local people make special trips just to have lunch or tea at their nearby National Trust house or garden.

By sitting down to enjoy a cup of tea and a sandwich, a scone or a biscuit, National Trust visitors are perpetuating a ritual that has its origins in Britain in the mid-17th century when tea started to arrive via Holland and Portugal, which had established trade routes to Japan and China a hundred years earlier. Merchants and aristocrats imported small amounts of tea into Britain in the 1650s, but it was Charles II's marriage in 1662 to a Portuguese princess, Catherine of Braganza, that established tea-drinking as an accepted practice. Catherine brought to London a 3lb (1.4kg) chest of tea as part of her dowry and she quickly introduced this to her friends at court. Regular consignments were soon being ordered for the King and Queen and tea drinking became a fashionable activity. Meanwhile, enterprising merchants, keen to increase sales of this new commodity, engaged in elaborate advertising campaigns, and gradually the trend spread. Tea was served, and loose tea sold, in the coffee houses that had sprung up in London and some provincial towns in the 1650s, but the high tax levied by Charles II meant that it was very expensive and therefore out of the reach of the working classes. Ale and gin continued to be the standard drinks of the majority of the population until 1784, when the tax was reduced from 119 per cent to 12 per cent (to 2½d. per lb) and tea overtook gin and ale in the popularity stakes. Had the tax remained, it is likely that the British would have ended up mainly drinking coffee like the French and Germans.

In the first half of the 18th century a powerful campaign against the coffee houses, which had become bawdy dens of iniquity, succeeded in closing them down, and, in their place, the pleasure gardens at Vauxhall, Chelsea, Marylebone, Islington, Bermondsey, Kentish Town and Kilburn provided family entertainment in London.

The price of entry to these gardens sometimes included tea with bread and butter, the idea being that, after enjoying rides on the river, horse-riding, listening to music or wandering through beautifully tended gardens, the family could relax and take some refreshment together. Sadly, the gardens survived for only a short time; by 1850 most had closed, but not before the ritual of afternoon tea had been firmly established as part of the British way of life. It is said to have been 'invented' in the early 19th century by Anna, wife of the 7th Duke of Bedford. Breakfast in those days was taken at nine or ten o'clock in the morning, and dinner, which had previously been eaten at two or three o'clock in the afternoon, was not until eight or nine o'clock. By four o'clock the Duchess, and no doubt others too, felt a little peckish; she therefore asked her footman to bring her all her tea-making equipage to her private room so that she could brew herself a pot of tea and enjoy it with a little light refreshment. The Duchess was so pleased with this arrangement that she started inviting her friends to join her, and soon all of London's elegant society was sipping 'afternoon tea' and gossiping all the while about people, places and events. With their tea they nibbled dainty sandwiches filled with ham or thinly sliced cucumber and with all the crusts cut off to make them prettier to look at and easier to eat. As the custom of taking tea became more popular, so the demand for teaware grew, and the potteries, silversmiths and furniture makers produced a wide range of tea services, cake plates, teaspoons, knives, strainers, teapots and kettles, caddies, caddy spoons and tea tables.

In 1884 the activities of the manageress of the London Bridge branch of the Aerated Bread Company (the ABC) brought afternoon tea out of the elegant salons of the aristocracy and into the realm of everyday middle- and working-class people. This enterprising lady, who was in the habit of offering a cup of tea and a chat to her regular customers when they came in to buy their loaves of bread, persuaded her employers to allow her to create a public tearoom on the premises. Other companies quickly followed suit and soon every high street had its ABC, Express Dairy, Lyons' or Kardomah tearoom. By the 1920s going out to tea was a pastime enjoyed by people from all classes and walks of life. Children who grew up during the Edwardian period have fond memories of tea out with nanny, and most people can remember their favourite tearooms with nostalgia and pleasure.

In the grander hotels and restaurants, tea dances became the craze from about 1912 onwards. A demonstration of the tango, which originated in the back streets of Buenos Aires, was given first in Paris and then in London. Initially couples danced between the restaurant tables, but, as the idea caught on, a space was cleared in the middle of the floor. Soon tango-teas and matinees were being held in most hotels and in half a dozen theatres around London. Books were written telling society hostesses how to organize tea dances, restaurants started tango-clubs, and dance teachers, such as Victor Silvester, made their fortunes. One well-known teacher of the time – Miss Gladys Beattie Crozier – wrote in her book *The Tango and How to Dance It*: 'What could be pleasanter on a dull wintry afternoon, at 5 o'clock or so, when calls or shopping are over, than to drop into one of the cheery little Thé Dansant clubs, which have sprung up all over the West End during the last month or two, to take one's place at a tiny table ... set forth with the prettiest of gold and white china, to enjoy a most elaborate and delicious tea served within a moment of one's arrival, while listening to an excellent string band playing delicious haunting airs'.

Sadly, the fashion for taking tea gradually dwindled, and the tea shops were replaced by fast-food chains with their plastic tables and convenience food.

In the mid-1980s, however, there was a revival of interest: new tea shops opened in unlikely places and quickly became popular; a rash of books about tea including teatime recipes appeared on bookshop shelves; tea dances again became the rage, even in provincial hotels and village halls; and going out for afternoon tea is now very much back in fashion. The National Trust tearooms have carried on regardless through the years of change, but here too there is a difference. The tearooms are expanding, a wider variety of cakes is being baked, and the tea served is now specially packaged for the Trust.

If you have always been a faithful drinker of good old 'British' tea, it is well worth experimenting with some of the speciality brews and blends.

What actually is tea? There are probably more than 10,000 different teas made around the world in more than 35 countries. All of them are made from the leaves and leaf buds of the tea bush, the white-flowered *Camellia sinensis*, a relative of the *Camellia japonica* that we grow in our gardens as a decorative shrub. There are two main varieties that are used to make tea – the *Camellia sinensis sinensis*, a native of China, and the *Camellia sinensis assamica*, a native of Assam in north-east India, and there are thousands of cultivars that have evolved over the centuries. Each of these grows differently depending on local conditions and each resulting tea will have a different character. Just as all wines vary according to the grape variety used, the growing situation and the manufacturing process used, so all teas vary according to the altitude at which the bushes grow, the seasonal changes, the amount of sunshine, the wind, frost, rainfall and temperature. And as with wines which are blended to give a standard quality and flavour, so teas are blended by the major blending companies to offer the consumer teas that taste the same each time the customer buys them. So your everyday teabag blend can and often does contain teas from Kenya, Malawi, Sri Lanka, India, Indonesia, Argentina and Brazil. The blender selects teas according to quality, taste, price, and the size and appearance of the leaf, and mixes them to give exactly the same taste and quality every time the tea is packed into teabags or cartons.

Just as wines are divided into categories such as white, red, rosé, sparkling and so on, so the many different types of tea are separated according to their manufacture and the main categories are white, green, oolong and black. White teas are made from the tightly furled buds of a particular varietal of the tea bush that pushes out plump buds covered with silvery-white hairs. After plucking, the buds are dried in the sun and packed. They give a pale, champagne-coloured liquor that has a soft, velvety, almost sweet flavour. Green teas are made from the leaves and leaf buds of the tea bush which, after picking, are either steamed or pan-fried to de-enzyme the leaf and then rolled or shaped by hand or machine. Some green teas have needle-like leaves that are dark green, flat and shiny. Gunpowder tea is made by rolling each individual leaf into a tiny ball that looks like a little pellet of lead shot, hence the name. Oolong teas are made by gently shaking or lightly rolling freshly picked and withered leaves and then allowing them to oxidize for a short time before drying. And black teas are made by picking, withering, rolling or chopping the green leaf before allowing it to fully oxidize until it turns to a deep amber brown. Drying in hot ovens removes almost all but 2–3% of the remaining water and the tea is sorted and packed, ready for delivery to the shops and supermarkets.

The most commonly drunk teas in the UK are Darjeeling with its lightly astringent, muscatel quality; Assam with a warm, woody, malty character; Ceylon teas from the island of Sri Lanka with their bright, brisk, golden flavour; English Breakfast-style teas that are made from Assam, Ceylon and African teas and offer a depth of flavour that marries well with strongly flavoured foods; smoky Lapsang Souchong from China, and Earl Grey, tea flavoured with essential oil of bergamot. Any white, green, oolong or black tea can be flavoured with fruits, flowers, spices and herbs to make what are called flavoured or scented teas. Although we traditionally add milk to our tea, many teas are better drunk without milk and it is always worth trying the liquor without milk first.

Although tea is drunk and enjoyed throughout the day, the favourite time for many people is at four or five o'clock in the afternoon, when the refreshing cuppa is often accompanied by a sweet or savoury treat. This book offers a wide selection of breads, scones, buns and biscuits served in National Trust tearooms and restaurants in England, Wales and Northern Ireland, as well as some traditional regional specialities. All are suitable fare for those who, in Samuel Johnson's words, may be 'a hardened and shameless tea-drinker, who has for twenty years diluted his meals with only the infusion of this fascinating plant; whose kettle has scarcely time to cool; who with tea amuses the evening, with tea solaces the midnight, and with tea welcomes the morning.'

CONVERSIONS

Weight	Liquid measure	Length	Temperature
15g (½oz)	15ml (½fl oz)	5mm (¼in)	110°C, 225°F, gas mark ¼
25g (1oz)	30ml (1fl oz)	1cm (½in)	120°C, 250°F, gas mark ½
40g (1½oz)	50ml (2fl oz)	1.5cm (⅝in)	140°C, 275°F, gas mark 1
55g (2oz)	75ml (2½fl oz)	2cm (¾in)	150°C, 300°F, gas mark 2
70g (2½oz)	100ml (3½fl oz)	2.5cm (1in)	160°C, 325°F, gas mark 3
85g (3oz)	125ml (4fl oz)	5cm (2in)	180°C, 350°F, gas mark 4
100g (3½oz)	150ml (5fl oz or ¼ pint)	7cm (2¾in)	190°C, 375°F, gas mark 5
115g (4oz)	200ml (7fl oz or ½ pint)	9cm (3½in)	200°C, 400°F, gas mark 6
125g (4½oz)	250ml (9fl oz)	10cm (4in)	220°C, 425°F, gas mark 7
140g (5oz)	300ml (10fl oz or ½ pint)	13cm (5in)	230°C, 450°F, gas mark 8
150g (5½oz)	350ml (12fl oz)	15cm (6in)	240°C, 475°F, gas mark 9
175g (6oz)	400ml (14fl oz)	18cm (7in)	
200g (7oz)	425ml (15fl oz or ¾ pint)	20cm (8in)	
225g (8oz)	500ml (18fl oz)	23cm (9in)	
250g (9oz)	600ml (20fl oz or 1 pint)	25cm (10in)	
300g (10½oz)		28cm (11in)	
350g (12oz)		30cm (12in)	
375g (13oz)			
400g (14oz)			
425g (15oz)			
450g (1lb)			
675g (1½lb)			
900g (2lb)			

AMERICAN EQUIVALENTS

Dry measures		
1 US cup	50g (¾oz)	breadcrumbs; cake crumbs
1 US cup	85g (3oz)	porridge or rolled oats
1 US cup	90g (3¼oz)	ground almonds; shredded coconut
1 US cup	100g (3½oz)	roughly chopped walnuts and other nuts; icing sugar; cocoa; drinking chocolate; flaked almonds; grated Cheddar cheese
1 US cup	150g (5½oz)	white flour; currants; rice flour; muesli; cornflour; chopped dates
1 US cup	175g (6oz)	wholemeal flour; oatmeal; raisins; sultanas; dried apricots; mixed candied peel
1 US cup	200g (7oz)	caster sugar; soft brown sugar; demerara sugar; rice; glacé cherries; semolina; chopped figs or plums
1 US cup	225g (8oz)	granulated sugar; curd cheese; cream cheese
1 US cup	300g (10½oz)	mincemeat; marmalade; jam
1 US cup	350g (12oz)	golden syrup; black treacle

Liquid measures		
⅛ US cup	30ml (1fl oz)	
¼ US cup	50ml (2fl oz)	
½ US cup	125ml (4fl oz)	
1 US cup	250ml (9fl oz)	
1¼ US cups	300ml (10fl oz)	
1¾ US cups	425ml (15fl oz)	
2 US cups	500ml (18fl oz)	
2½ US cups	600ml (20fl oz)	

Measures for fats		
¼ stick	25g (1oz)	
1 stick	100g (3½oz)	
(½ US cup)		

BREADS

When tea was first served in England in the 17th century and for the 150 years or so of domestic tea-drinking, the only food served with tea was elegantly thin slices of bread and butter. As afternoon tea became more and more important during the 19th century, fresh breads played an important part on the tea table in the form of neat, crustless sandwiches filled with chicken, egg mayonnaise, baked ham, thinly sliced cucumber and smoked salmon. Today, ubiquitous plastic packs of dull white and brown breads leave us yearning for the flavour and texture of days gone by.

ORGANIC WHOLEWHEAT BREAD

This lovely nutty-flavoured bread comes from Branscombe Bakery, the last traditional bakery in Devon. Until 1987 it was run by brothers Gerald and Stuart Collier who baked bread, buns, cakes, tarts and scones every day of the year. The oven was lit at four o'clock every morning and then, three hours later when it had reached the required temperature, the ashes were raked out, the oven cleaned and then the first batch of 130 loaves arranged inside.

25g (1oz) fresh yeast (to substitute dried yeast, see page 85)

½ teaspoon light or dark soft brown sugar

600–750ml (1–1¼ pints) warm water (it should be almost hand-hot, and the amount needed varies according to the flour used)

900g (2lb) organic wholemeal flour, sifted and warmed slightly in the oven

1 tablespoon sea salt

1 tablespoon corn or sunflower oil

1 tablespoon clear honey

Makes 2 x 900g (2lb) loaves

Cream together the yeast and sugar and blend with 50–75ml (2–3fl oz) of the warm water. Leave in a warm, draught-free place for 10–20 minutes until frothy – there should be at least 1.5cm (¾in) of froth on the top. Mix together the flour and salt and make a well in the middle. Pour in the oil, honey, yeast mixture and enough of the remaining water to give a soft, elastic dough. Knead by hand for about 10 minutes. Shape the dough into a ball and place in a lightly greased bowl. Dust the top with a little flour, cover with a clean, damp cloth and leave in a warm, draught-free place until almost doubled in size (this can take anything from 50 minutes to 2 hours). Grease two 900g (2lb) loaf tins. Turn the dough out on to a lightly floured board and knead vigorously for 8–10 minutes. Divide the dough into two equal portions and shape to fit the tins. Place in the tins, sprinkle the tops with a little more flour and cover with a clean, damp cloth. Leave in a warm place for a further 30–40 minutes until the dough reaches the top of the tins. Meanwhile heat the oven to 220°C, 425°F, gas mark 7. When the dough has risen, bake the loaves for 30 minutes. Remove from the oven and remove from the tins. Place the loaves in the oven for a further 10–15 minutes until they sound hollow when tapped. Remove from the oven and cool on a wire rack.

BATEMAN'S SODA BREAD

A soft, light bread, this recipe is from Rudyard Kipling's Jacobean house in East Sussex.

225g (8oz) plain wholemeal
    flour, sifted
2 teaspoons baking powder
½ teaspoon salt
1 teaspoon demerara sugar
25g (1oz) butter, softened
150ml (5fl oz) milk
Cracked wheat, oatmeal or oats

Makes 1 x 15cm (6in) round loaf

Preheat the oven to 200°C, 400°F, gas mark 6. Grease a baking tray. Mix together the flour, baking powder, salt and sugar and rub in the butter. Add the milk and mix to a soft dough. Shape into a round and place on the prepared tray. Brush the top with a little milk and sprinkle with cracked wheat, oatmeal or oats. Bake for 20–30 minutes until well risen and browned. Remove from the oven and serve warm with butter.

HERB BREAD

This recipe comes from Cliveden in Buckinghamshire, which was built in 1850–51 for the Duke and Duchess of Sutherland, great friends of Queen Victoria who of course loved tea and teatime.

225g (8oz) self-raising white or
   wholemeal flour (or a
   mixture of half and half),
   sifted
1 teaspoon dry English
   mustard powder
2 tablespoons fresh chopped
   herbs (chives, thyme, basil,
   sage, parsley)
100g (4oz) mature Cheddar
   cheese, grated
25g (1oz) butter
1 egg, beaten
150ml (5fl oz) water

Makes 1 x 450g (1lb) loaf

Preheat the oven to 190°C, 375°F, gas mark 5. Grease a 450g (1lb) loaf tin. Mix together the flour, mustard, herbs and cheese. Melt the butter, add to the mixture with the egg and water and mix to a soft, wet, cake-like dough. Turn into the prepared tin and bake for 45 minutes until well risen and golden brown. Remove from the oven and cool on a wire rack. Serve warm or cold with butter.

Right: Herb Bread.

BUTTERMILK OATEN BREAD

Fine oatmeal gives a wonderful gritty texture to this favourite Irish bread. Buttermilk was once a staple ingredient in breads and cakes, and gave a slightly sour taste and good keeping qualities. Serve this as a satisfying part of 'high tea', warm with cheese or toasted with melting butter and thick fruity jams.

200g (7oz) fine oatmeal
300ml (10fl oz) buttermilk
125ml (4fl oz) milk
250g (9oz) plain flour, sifted
1 teaspoon baking powder
¼ teaspoon salt

Makes 2 small loaves

Soak the oatmeal in the buttermilk and milk overnight. The following day, preheat the oven to 180°C, 350°F, gas mark 4. Grease a baking tray. Mix together the flour, baking powder and salt. Add the oatmeal and milk mixture and mix well to give a soft dough. Knead until smooth. Divide into two portions and, on a floured board, roll each portion out to a thickness of about 2.5cm (1in) and about 10cm (4in) in diameter. Place both loaves on the prepared tray and bake for 35–40 minutes until they are golden and sound hollow when tapped. Remove from the oven and serve hot with butter.

Left: Buttermilk Oaten Bread.

SESAME ROLLS

From Trerice in Cornwall, these little rolls enjoy the sweet nuttiness of sesame and are delicious at teatime filled with smoked salmon or honey-roast ham. The glory of Trerice is the south-facing drawing room – a perfect room in which to take tea. Displayed here are some fine examples of Chinese porcelain that were imported on the same ships that brought the chests of tea from the Orient.

15g (½oz) fresh yeast (to substitute dried yeast, see page 85)
2 teaspoons caster sugar
400ml (15fl oz) water, warmed
675g (1½lb) strong plain white flour, sifted
1½ teaspoons full-cream milk powder (Coffeemate or similar)
½ teaspoon salt
25g (1oz) butter, softened
1 egg, beaten, mixed with a little water
2–3 tablespoons sesame seeds

Makes approximately 14 rolls

Mix together the yeast, sugar and 75ml (3fl oz) of the water. Leave in a warm place for about 20–30 minutes until frothy. Mix together the flour, milk powder and salt and rub in the fat. Add the yeast mixture and the remaining water and mix to a pliable dough. Knead until smooth and elastic, then place in a bowl, cover with a damp cloth and leave in a warm place for 1–1½ hours until doubled in size. Grease two baking trays. When the dough is well risen, divide into 65g (2½oz) pieces, form these into bun shapes and place on the prepared trays. Brush the tops with egg wash and sprinkle liberally with sesame seeds. Leave in a warm place for about 30 minutes until well risen. Meanwhile heat the oven to 200°C, 400°F, gas mark 6. When the rolls are well risen, bake for 20–25 minutes until golden brown and firm. Remove from the oven and lift on to a wire rack to cool. Serve warm or cold.

If liked, stir a tablespoon of sesame seeds into the dough with the yeast mixture. Sprinkle as above with more seeds before baking.

KENTISH HUFFKINS

Huffkins were traditionally baked in the kitchens of Kentish farms and carried out to the hop fields to feed the bands of seasonal workers from the East End of London who arrived each year for their annual working holiday. The indented middle of each huffkin was usually filled with stewed cherries or apples from the nearby orchards.

450g (1lb) plain flour, sifted
½ teaspoon salt
25g (1oz) lard, softened
25g (1oz) fresh yeast (to
    substitute dried yeast,
    see page 85)
1 teaspoon caster sugar
350ml (12fl oz) milk, or a
    mixture of milk and water,
    warmed

Makes 12 huffkins

Grease two baking trays. Sift together the flour and salt and rub in the lard. Cream the yeast with the sugar and add to the warmed milk (or milk and water). Add to the flour and mix to a light, soft dough. Leave in a warm place for about 1 hour until doubled in size. On a floured board, knead the dough lightly, then divide into twelve flat oval cakes about 1cm (½in) thick. Place on the prepared trays and leave in a warm place for about 30 minutes until well risen. Meanwhile, heat the oven to 200°C, 400°F, gas mark 6. When the huffkins are well risen, make a hole with your thumb in the middle of each and bake for 10–20 minutes until lightly browned and firm. Remove from the oven and cover immediately with a clean, dry cloth until cold; this helps to keep the rolls soft.

BOXTY BREAD

Boxty bread is traditional festive Irish bread, flat and round and marked into four portions before baking to allow for easy division once cooked. With potatoes its essentially Irish ingredient, it was once an indulgence for Shrove Tuesday, All Saints' Day or Hallowe'en.

225g (8oz) raw potatoes
225g (8oz) mashed potatoes
225g (8oz) plain flour, sifted
50g (2oz) butter, melted
Salt and freshly ground
    black pepper

Makes 2 small round flat loaves

Preheat the oven to 190°C, 375°F, gas mark 5. Grease a baking tray. Wash and peel the raw potatoes. Grate into a clean cloth and wring well over a bowl to squeeze out the juice. Place the grated potatoes in a bowl with the mashed potatoes and mix well together. Leave the starchy liquid in the bowl until the starch has settled, then pour off the liquid and add the starch to the potatoes. Add the flour, melted butter and seasoning and mix to a soft dough. Knead well. Divide into two portions and, on a floured board, roll into flat rounds. Place on the baking tray and divide the top of each loaf into four with a sharp knife. Bake for 40 minutes until firm and golden. Remove from the oven and serve hot with plenty of butter.

RAISIN AND BRAN BREAD

A low-fat tea bread, this is made to a recipe from Standen, the Sussex Arts and Crafts home designed by Philip Webb, one of William Morris' closest friends. This was almost the last house he ever built but some of the same features he used in his original commission, Morris' Red House, are echoed in its architecture. At the time the house was built in the 1890s, interior design was heavily influenced by oriental style and on show in the drawing room is a delicate Japanese tea service.

75g (3oz) bran cereal (All Bran
   or similar)
75g (3oz) sugar
175g (6oz) raisins
300ml (10fl oz) milk
175g (6oz) wholemeal
   self-raising flour, sifted
50–75ml (2–3fl oz) milk
   and water mixed in
   equal measures

Makes 1 x 900g (2lb) loaf

Put the bran cereal, sugar, raisins and milk into a bowl and leave overnight (or for at least 6 hours), stirring occasionally if possible. Preheat the oven to 160°C, 325°F, gas mark 3. Grease and line a 900g (2lb) loaf tin. Add the flour to the soaked ingredients and mix with enough of the milk and water to give a runny consistency. Pour into the prepared tin and bake for 1 hour. Remove from the oven and leave to cool in the tin.

The bran gives this bread a pleasant, rather coarse texture. It contains very little fat and sugar and is therefore ideal for anybody who is concerned about cholesterol or calories.

DERBYSHIRE SPICED EASTER FRUIT BREAD

Many of our traditional fruited celebration cakes originated as plain bread mixtures that were enriched for special occasions with dried fruit, cream, spices and butter – all of which were too expensive to use every day. This Easter bread is a perfect example of readily available ingredients such as flour, lard and milk combined with more costly dates, sultanas, sugar and cinnamon.

225g (8oz) self-raising flour,
   sifted
1 teaspoon mixed spice
½ teaspoon ground cinnamon
75g (3oz) lard, softened
75g (3oz) sugar
50g (2oz) sultanas
50g (2oz) dates, chopped
1 egg, beaten
6 tablespoons milk

Makes 1 x 900g (2lb) loaf

Preheat the oven to 190°C, 375°F, gas mark 5. Grease and line a 900g (2lb) loaf tin. Mix together the flour and spices. Chop the lard into very small pieces and cut roughly into the flour with a knife. Add the sugar, sultanas, dates, egg and milk and mix to a soft consistency. Turn into the prepared tin and bake for 40–45 minutes until a skewer comes out clean. Remove from the oven and turn out on to a wire rack to cool. Serve sliced with butter.

DATE AND WALNUT LOAF

This Cornish recipe from Cotehele in Cornwall is typical in its use of spices, brown sugar and exotic fruit. From the 17th century, ships from the Orient imported such luxuries through the Cornish ports. Cotehele would certainly have known about such ingredients, sitting as it does close to the River Tamar, which for centuries was the only effective route to the outside world. The immense oven in the north wall of the kitchen almost certainly baked a number of these loaves over the centuries.

225g (8oz) self-raising flour,
    sifted
50g (2oz) whole walnuts
1 teaspoon mixed spice
75g (3oz) butter, softened
100g (4oz) light or dark soft
    brown sugar
225g (8oz) whole dates
150ml (5fl oz) water
2 eggs, beaten
2 tablespoons sesame seeds

Makes 1 x 900g (2lb) loaf

Preheat the oven to 180°C, 350°F, gas mark 4. Grease and line a 900g (2lb) loaf tin. Mix together the flour, walnuts and mixed spice. Place the butter, sugar, dates and water in a pan and bring gently to the boil. Remove from the heat and cool for a few minutes. Add to the flour, spice and nuts with the beaten eggs and beat well. Turn into the prepared tin, hollow the middle a little and sprinkle the top with the sesame seeds. Bake for 1–1¼ hours until a skewer comes out clean. Remove from the oven and turn out on to a wire rack to cool. Serve sliced with butter.

ORANGE GINGERBREAD

In Britain's past, gingerbreads and ginger biscuits were sold at medieval fairs and were often made in special shapes for different locations. In Hampshire, Gingerbread Husbands were popular, while in Bath, heart-shaped Gingerbread Valentines were sold. Some were soft cakes served in slices while others were crunchy biscuits. This orange version comes from Bateman's in Sussex where Rudyard Kipling perhaps took tea with a slice of gingerbread in the entrance hall – the favourite setting for afternoon tea.

100g (4oz) butter
100g (4oz) black treacle
100g (4oz) golden syrup
50g (2oz) light or dark soft
    brown sugar
1 teaspoon bicarbonate of soda
150ml (5fl oz) orange juice
225g (8oz) plain wholemeal
    flour, sifted
1 heaped teaspoon mixed spice
2 heaped teaspoons ground
    ginger
2 eggs, beaten
40g (1½oz) flaked almonds to
    decorate

Makes 12 pieces

Preheat the oven to 150°C, 300°F, gas mark 2. Grease and line an 18 x 28cm (7 x 11in) Swiss roll tin. In a medium-sized pan melt together the butter, treacle, syrup and sugar over a low heat. Dissolve the bicarbonate of soda in the orange juice and add to the mixture. Stir well. Add the flour, spice, ginger and beaten eggs and beat well to a smooth batter. Pour into the prepared tin and scatter the flaked almonds over the top. Bake for 1 hour until firm and well risen. Remove from the oven and leave to cool in the tin. When cold, cut into bars and lift carefully from the tin.

SWEET WHOLEMEAL BANNOCK

Irish teatimes demanded all the same treats as were enjoyed throughout Britain from about 1840 when Anna Maria, 7th Duchess of Bedford, is said to have named the mid-afternoon indulgence of a pot of tea and a little something to eat. During the first 200 years of tea drinking in England, the only food offered with tea had been thin slices of bread and butter, but once afternoon tea and high tea became popular during the 19th century, the tea-time menu gradually became more elaborate.

350g (12oz) plain wholemeal
    flour, sifted
100g (4oz) plain white flour,
    sifted
1 teaspoon bicarbonate of soda
50g (2oz) butter, softened
2 dessertspoons caster sugar
200ml (7fl oz) buttermilk

Makes 1 x 900g (2lb) loaf or
1 x 20cm (8in) round bannock

Preheat the oven to 180°C, 350°F, gas mark 4. Grease and line a 900g (2lb) loaf tin or a 20cm (8in) round tin. Mix together the flours and bicarbonate of soda and rub in the butter. Add the sugar and mix with the buttermilk to give a soft, pliable dough. Knead lightly, then shape to fit the tin. Place in the tin and bake for 35–45 minutes until well risen and golden. Remove from the oven and turn out on to a wire rack to cool. Serve warm, sliced and spread with butter.

HONEY TEA BREAD

This recipe comes from Kingston Lacy in Devon, where the drawing room is laid out as it was in 1900 and includes a silver tea service on a tray with a kettle standing over its little burner. Since tea was, until the late 19th century, a very expensive commodity, the lady of the house never allowed her servants to brew the tea but took charge herself of the leaf, the kettle and the teapot. The locked tea caddy was kept in the drawing room away from the potential pilfering of the housemaids.

FOR THE LOAF
225g (8oz) mixed dried fruit
150ml (5fl oz) cold tea
100g (4oz) clear honey
225g (8oz) self-raising flour,
    sifted
1 egg, well beaten
100g (4oz) butter, melted

FOR THE TOPPING
1 tablespoon honey, warmed
25g (1oz) finely chopped nuts
    (walnuts, hazelnuts or
    almonds)
25g (1oz) demerara sugar

Makes 1 x 900g (2lb) loaf

Place the dried fruit, tea and honey in a bowl and leave to soak overnight or for at least 6 hours. Preheat the oven to 150°C, 300°F, gas mark 2. Grease and line a 900g (2lb) loaf tin. Mix the flour into the fruit mixture. Add the beaten egg and beat hard. Finally, beat in the melted butter. Turn into the prepared tin and bake for 50 minutes. Remove from the oven and prepare the topping. Brush with the warmed honey, mix together the nuts and sugar and sprinkle over the top. Return to the oven and bake for a further 15–20 minutes until a skewer comes out clean. Remove from the oven and leave to cool in the tin. When cool, carefully remove from the tin and serve sliced with butter.

SAFFRON CAKE

In the 14th century, vast fields of blue crocuses were grown in Essex to produce home-grown saffron. But when saffron began to feature among the exotic goods being imported to England through ports along the Cornish coast, the trade moved to the West Country. Cornwall is rich in recipes for saffron buns, cakes and fruit loaves that were particularly popular during Lent, at Easter and as fairings at annual fairs. This is another Cotehele recipe.

15g (½oz) fresh yeast (to substitute dried yeast, see page 85)

32g (1¼oz) caster sugar

175ml (6fl oz) water, warmed

7g (¼oz) low-fat freeze-dried milk powder

250g (9oz) strong plain white flour, sifted

7g (¼oz) saffron, ground and soaked for several hours in 2 teaspoons warm water

Generous pinch of salt

65g (2½ oz) butter, softened

65–75g (2½–3oz) currants

40–50g (1½–2oz) mixed candied peel

Makes 1 x 900g (2lb) loaf

Cream together the yeast and caster sugar and mix with the warm water, milk powder and 25g (1oz) of the flour. Whisk, then leave in a warm place for 30 minutes until frothy and doubled in size. Strain the saffron, add with all the other ingredients to the yeast mixture and beat well to a fairly elastic dough. Leave in a warm place for a further 40–50 minutes until doubled in size. Grease a 900g (2lb) loaf tin. Turn the mixture into the tin and stand in a warm place for 30 minutes to rise almost to the top of the tin. Meanwhile, heat the oven to 180°C, 350°F, gas mark 4. When the dough has risen, bake for 50 minutes to 1 hour until a skewer comes out clean. Remove from the oven and turn out on to a wire rack to cool. This saffron loaf is not very sweet and, spread with butter and honey or your chosen preserve, it makes an ideal tea bread.

RIPON CHRISTMAS BREAD

Another traditional enriched bread dough, this festive loaf from Yorkshire includes allspice in the ingredients. Also called Jamaican Pepper or newspice, it is the dried unripe fruit of the Pimenta dioica plant. Its aroma and taste combines the complex characters of cinnamon and cloves and adds a slightly hotter, peppery quality.

FOR THE BASIC BREAD DOUGH

900g (2lb) plain flour, sifted
2 teaspoons salt
25g (1oz) fresh yeast (to substitute dried yeast, see page 85)
1 teaspoon caster sugar
100g (4oz) butter, softened
600ml (1 pint) milk, warmed

FOR THE ADDITIONAL FLAVOURING

175g (6oz) lard, softened and cut into small pieces
100g (4oz) raisins
50g (2oz) mixed candied peel
100g (4oz) granulated or caster sugar
225g (8oz) currants
½ teaspoon allspice

Makes 2 x 900g (2lb) loaves

First make the basic bread dough. Mix together the flour and salt. Cream the yeast with the sugar. Rub the fat into the flour, add the yeast and warm milk and mix to a light dough. Knead well with floured hands until smooth. Place the dough in a bowl and stand in a warm place for 1½–2 hours until doubled in size. Grease two 900g (2lb) loaf tins. Mix together all the additional ingredients and work into the dough until all are evenly distributed. Divide the mixture between the tins and leave in a warm place until the dough almost reaches the top of the tins. Meanwhile, heat the oven to 160°C, 325°F, gas mark 3. When the loaves are well risen, bake for approximately 2 hours until golden and firm. Remove from the oven and turn out on to a wire rack to cool. Serve either warm or cold and spread with butter.

In most areas of Britain in the past, large batches of fruit loaves were baked at Christmas ready to feed the family and any visitors who called at the house between Christmas and New Year.

BLACKBERRY TEA BREAD

Made with freshly harvested hedgerow berries, this tea loaf from Trelissick in Cornwall makes a delicious change from more traditional fruited breads. The garden here was created by Ronald Copeland who was chairman, and later managing director, of the Spode china factory. Many of the flowers that flourish in the mild Cornish air were the inspiration for the floral designs produced at the works.

350g (12oz) plain flour, sifted
1 teaspoon mixed spice
175g (6oz) butter, softened
175g (6oz) caster sugar
225g (8oz) fresh or frozen
    blackberries (if frozen, use
    straight from the freezer)
Grated rind and juice of
    1 lemon
1 tablespoon black treacle
2 eggs, beaten
½ teaspoon bicarbonate of soda
2 tablespoons milk

Makes 1 x 900g (2lb) loaf

Preheat the oven to 180°C, 350°F, gas mark 4. Grease and line a 900g (2lb) loaf tin. Mix together the flour and mixed spice and rub in the butter until the mixture bears a resemblance to fine breadcrumbs. Add the sugar, blackberries, lemon rind and juice, treacle and eggs and mix well. Dissolve the bicarbonate of soda in the milk, add to the mixture and beat well. Pour into the prepared tin, level and bake for 45 minutes. Reduce the oven temperature to 150°C, 300°F, gas mark 2 and cook for a further 30–45 minutes until a skewer comes out clean. Remove from the oven and leave in the tin for about 15 minutes before turning out on to a wire rack to cool.

This unusual loaf is an ideal and novel way of using the blackberries that flourish in our hedgerows every summer.

ORANGE TEA BREAD

This recipe is from Moseley Old Hall in Staffordshire, where Charles II hid from Parliamentarian soldiers after the Royalist defeat at the Battle of Worcester in 1651. After his return to England, he married Catherine of Braganza, who introduced tea to the English court. Born in Portugal, Catherine was an avid tea-drinker long before the English had even heard of the drink, and when she arrived in England in 1662 for her wedding she brought a chest of tea with her, served it to her friends and set a new fashion.

75g (3oz) butter, softened
225g (8oz) self-raising flour
   (white or wholemeal), sifted
75g (3oz) caster sugar
50g (2oz) walnuts, roughly
   chopped
1 large egg, beaten
2 oranges (the grated rind of
   both, the juice from one
   and the other left whole)
2 tablespoons caster sugar for
   sprinkling

Makes 1 x 900g (2lb) loaf

Preheat the oven to 180°C, 350°F, gas mark 4. Grease and line a 900g (2lb) loaf tin. Rub the butter into the flour until the mixture resembles fine breadcrumbs. Stir in the sugar and walnuts. Add the egg, orange rind and juice and beat well. Turn into the prepared tin. Holding the remaining orange over the tin so as to catch any juice, remove the skin and pith and divide into segments. Arrange over the top of the cake and sprinkle with the caster sugar. Bake for 1¼–1½ hours until a skewer comes out clean. Remove from the oven and leave to cool in the tin.

BARM BRACK

Another good example of the use of succulent dried fruits and candied peel to make a plain cake more interesting. Barm means 'leaven' or 'yeast' and brack means 'speckled', referring to the fruit scattered through the dough. Barm brack was often made in flattened rounds and is served sliced, sometimes toasted and spread with plenty of butter.

100g (4oz) currants
100g (4oz) sultanas
100g (4oz) raisins
50g (2oz) mixed candied peel
50g (2oz) glacé cherries,
    quartered
200g (7oz) light soft brown
    sugar
300ml (10fl oz) cold black tea
Grated rind of 1 lemon
2 eggs, beaten
250g (9oz) self-raising flour,
    sifted
1 teaspoon mixed spice
Pinch of salt

Makes 1 x 900g (2lb) loaf

Put the dried fruit, glace cherries and candied peel into a bowl with the sugar, tea and lemon rind and leave to soak for at least 3 hours, preferably longer. Preheat the oven to 180°C, 350°F, gas mark 4. Grease and line a 900g (2lb) loaf tin. Add the eggs, flour, mixed spice and salt to the fruit mixture and mix thoroughly. Turn into the prepared tin and bake for 1½–1¾ hours until a skewer comes out clean. Remove from the oven and turn out on to a wire rack to cool. Serve sliced with butter.

BARA BRITH

Bara Brith is the traditional tea loaf of Wales, easy to prepare and delicious sliced and spread with butter. This recipe comes from Erddig, a great Georgian house visited on 16th August 1921 by Queen Mary, who took afternoon tea in the dining room after touring the ground-floor rooms and visiting the servants' hall. Perhaps she ate Bara Brith in true Welsh style that day!

350g (12oz) mixed dried fruit
350ml (12fl oz) red wine
100g (4oz) butter
100g (4oz) light soft brown
  sugar
50ml (2fl oz) milk
1 tablespoon black treacle
225g (8oz) self-raising flour,
  sifted
1 teaspoon mixed spice
2 eggs, beaten

Makes 1 x 900g (2lb) loaf

Soak the fruit in the red wine overnight. The next day preheat the oven to 180°C, 350°F, gas mark 4. Grease and line a 900g (2lb) loaf tin. Add the butter, sugar, milk and treacle to the fruit, bring to the boil and simmer for 5 minutes. Remove from the heat and leave to cool. Add the flour, mixed spice and beaten eggs and beat well with a wooden spoon. Turn into the prepared tin and bake just below the middle of the oven for 1–1¼ hours until a skewer comes out clean. Remove from the oven and leave to cool in the tin for 15 minutes before turning out on to a wire rack to cool completely. Serve sliced with butter.

Each region has its own version of this traditional Welsh tea bread. This one may be made with cold tea instead of red wine.

Right: Bara Brith.
Next page: Barm Brack.

SUFFOLK FOURSES

During the harvest each year in England's eastern counties, the farmers' wives worked hard to produce four or five meals a day to feed the hungry local and itinerant workers. Flasks of tea and bottles of cold homemade lemonade were carried out in bags and baskets by the women and children for the midday and mid-afternoon meals. Everyone stopped work, found somewhere to rest in the shade of a nearby haystack and devoured the freshly baked breads, rolls and cakes. This currant bread would have been on the menu.

25g (1oz) fresh yeast (to
    substitute dried yeast,
    see page 85)
1 teaspoon caster sugar
300ml (10fl oz) milk
900g (2lb) plain flour, sifted
½ teaspoon salt
50g (2oz) lard, softened
100g (4oz) caster, granulated
    or demerara sugar
100g (4oz) currants or raisins
Pinch of mixed spice
175g (6oz) butter
3 eggs, well beaten
Caster or demerara sugar
    for dusting

Makes approximately 16 cakes

Cream the yeast with the teaspoon of caster sugar. Warm the milk and add to the yeast. Mix together the flour and salt and rub in the fat. Add the sugar, currants or raisins and spice and mix well. Melt the butter and stir into the beaten eggs. Add to the milk and yeast mixture and pour into the flour. Mix with a round-bladed knife to a light dough. Cover the bowl with a clean, damp cloth and leave in a warm place for about 2 hours until the dough has doubled in size. Meanwhile grease two baking trays. When the dough has risen, knead on a lightly floured board, then roll out to a thickness of approximately 1.5cm (¾in) and cut into rounds 10cm (4in) in diameter. Place on the prepared trays and leave to rise in a warm place for 30 minutes. Meanwhile heat the oven to 200°C, 400°F, gas mark 6. When the fourses have risen, mark the tops into four sections and dust with caster or demerara sugar. Bake for 15–20 minutes until firm and golden. Remove from the oven and eat either warm or cold, split and buttered.

Left: Suffolk Fourses.
Previous page: Cheese and Celery Whirls.

CHEESE AND CELERY WHIRLS

This recipe comes from Longshaw Estate in South Yorkshire, where homemade breads would have taken an important place on the 'high tea' table. Workers in the nearby quarries and mills would have been ravenous when they returned home at 5.30pm and so tucked into meat pies, thick slices of ham, chunks of cheese and home-baked breads and cakes – all washed down with several cups of strong black tea with milk and sugar.

350g (12oz) self-raising flour, sifted

1 teaspoon salt

½ teaspoon dry English mustard powder

50g (2oz) butter, softened

100g (4oz) mature Cheddar cheese, grated

1 garlic clove (or more to taste), crushed

1 egg, beaten

150ml (5fl oz) milk

3–4 sticks of celery, washed and roughly chopped

Makes approximately 10–12 whirls

Preheat the oven to 220°C, 425°F, gas mark 7. Mix together the flour, salt and mustard powder. Rub in the butter until the mixture resembles breadcrumbs. Add most of the grated cheese (reserving a little for sprinkling on top), garlic, beaten egg and milk and mix well so that all the ingredients are evenly distributed. On a floured board, knead lightly and then roll out to a rectangle approximately 23 x 30cm (9 x 12in). Scatter the celery over the surface. Roll up like a Swiss roll, starting with the narrow edge. Cut slices approximately 1.5cm (½in) thick, lay them flat on the prepared baking trays and sprinkle a little of the remaining cheese over the surface of each. Bake for 15–20 minutes until golden and well risen. Remove from the oven and serve warm.

These pretty whirls make an excellent accompaniment to a dinner party starter or they are suitable served as a teatime savoury. They are beautifully light and extremely tasty.

BOX HILL BREAD PUDDING

Bread pudding, popular since the 1300s and a real favourite in the 1940s and 50s, was the cook's way of using up stale bread and so it was often called 'poor man's pudding'. Dried fruits, spices, sugar, eggs and milk were added to soften the dry dough and make it more palatable. Another way of using up leftover bread was to make bread-and-butter pudding or Queen of Puddings, a soft, rather sloppy mix of bread and milk, a layer of jam and a frothy meringue topping.

450g (1lb) bread (white, brown
    or a mixture)
225g (8oz) raisins or currants
100g (4oz) glacé cherries,
    cut in half
100g (4oz) shredded suet
100g (4oz) caster sugar
2 teaspoons grated nutmeg
1 teaspoon ground cinnamon
2 eggs, beaten
Milk for mixing

Makes 16 slabs

Break the bread into small pieces, cover with cold water and leave to soak for at least 1 hour.

Preheat the oven to 160°C, 325°F, gas mark 3. Grease a shallow baking tin approximately 20 x 30cm (8 x 12in). Strain and squeeze as much water as possible out of the bread and beat to break up any lumps. Add the dried fruit, cherries, suet, sugar, spices and eggs and beat together, adding enough milk to give a soft, dropping consistency. Pour into the prepared tin and bake for 1½–2 hours until firm. Remove from the oven and leave to cool in the tin. When cold, cut into slabs. This traditional fruit cake is adapted from Mrs Beeton's original recipe.

BISCUITS

Favourite crunchy fairings and cookies, and soft, crumbly shortbreads often have historic connections to pagan celebrations, fairs, high days and holidays. Today, these quick and easy-to-make recipes offer a satisfying alternative to shop-bought teatime nibbles.

CORNISH FAIRINGS

At fairgrounds in the past, travelling salesmen often sold little bags of delicacies containing such things as spiced biscuits, caraway comfits, candied angelica, macaroons and almond sweetmeats. Gradually, over the years, the cakes and biscuits were sold as separate items and became known as fairings. This recipe is for the traditional spicy biscuits.

100g (4oz) butter
100g (4oz) granulated sugar
100g (4oz) golden syrup
225g (8oz) plain flour, sifted
1 teaspoon baking powder
1 teaspoon bicarbonate of soda
1 teaspoon ground ginger
1 teaspoon mixed spice
1 teaspoon ground cinnamon

Makes approximately
26 biscuits

Preheat the oven to 150°C, 300°F, gas mark 2. Grease two or three baking trays. Put the butter, sugar and syrup into a small pan and melt gently together until the sugar is dissolved. Mix together the dry ingredients and add the sugar mixture. Mix to a soft dough. Form the dough into balls weighing approximately 22g ($^3/_4$oz) and place on the prepared trays, leaving plenty of room for the biscuits to spread while cooking. Press each ball down lightly and bake for 10–15 minutes until golden. Remove from the oven and leave to cool on the trays for 5 minutes before lifting carefully on to a wire rack to cool completely.

ABBEYS

Sometimes the enjoyment of a cup of tea is enhanced by the addition of a small sweet treat, and these biscuits are perfect. With their chocolate coating, they combine well with a strong tea such as Kenya, Assam or a robust English Breakfast. English breakfast blends are usually made up of a mixture of teas from Assam in north-east India, Ceylon from the southern central mountains of the island of Sri Lanka, and African teas from Kenya or Malawi.

FOR THE BISCUITS
100g (4oz) butter, softened
100g (4oz) caster sugar
1 teaspoon golden syrup
100g (4oz) self-raising flour,
   sifted
100g (4oz) porridge oats
½ tablespoon full-cream milk
   powder (Coffeemate or
   similar)
½ teaspoon bicarbonate of soda

FOR THE COATING
275g (10oz) plain or milk
   chocolate

Makes 16 biscuits

Preheat the oven to 150°C, 300°F, gas mark 2. Grease two baking trays. Beat together the butter, sugar and syrup until light and fluffy. Add the other ingredients and work together. Form the mixture into balls weighing approximately 25g (1oz) and place on the prepared trays. Press down slightly with the palm of the hand and bake for 20 minutes until pale golden. Remove from the oven and leave to cool on the trays for a few minutes before lifting on to a wire rack to cool completely. Melt the chocolate in a narrow but deep container (a cup or small bowl) and dip the biscuits into the chocolate so that half of each biscuit is coated. Place carefully on the wire rack or on greaseproof paper and leave to set.

These are excellent served with ice-cream or other light desserts, as well as being perfect with morning coffee or afternoon tea.

DEVON FLATS

An important traditional ingredient in these little biscuits is Devonshire clotted cream, which is today manufactured in commercial dairies. But before mechanization, it was made in the individual dairy of each large farm or country house, where fresh, creamy milk was left to stand for 24 hours to settle. It was then gently heated until a thick layer of cream formed on the surface and was skimmed off ready to be eaten piled on to puddings, desserts and freshly baked scones.

225g (8oz) self-raising flour, sifted
Pinch of salt
100g (4oz) caster sugar
100ml (4fl oz) clotted or double cream
1 egg, beaten
1 tablespoon fresh milk

Makes 24 flats

Preheat the oven to 220°C, 425°F, gas mark 7. Grease two baking trays. Mix together the flour, salt and sugar. Add the cream, beaten egg and enough milk to give a stiff dough. On a lightly floured board, roll out to a thickness of approximately 0.75cm (⅜in) and cut into circles using a 7.5cm (3in) cutter. Place on the prepared trays and bake for 8–10 minutes until golden. Remove from the oven and lift carefully on to a wire rack to cool.

LINZER BISCUITS

Originally from Linz in Austria, these spiced biscuits were traditionally made with almonds and lemon. Two biscuits are sandwiched together with jam (always blackcurrant in the past but today more commonly raspberry or apricot) and sometimes the lower layer was covered with a lattice top or the hole was only cut in the top biscuit, allowing the rich colour of the jammy middle to show through.

275g (10oz) self-raising flour, sifted
Generous pinch of ground cinnamon
Generous pinch of ground cloves
225g (8oz) butter, softened
175g (6oz) caster sugar
1 egg, beaten
5–6 tablespoons raspberry or apricot jam

Makes approximately 25 double biscuits

Preheat the oven to 160°C, 325°F, gas mark 3. Grease two or three baking trays. Mix together all the ingredients except the jam to make a soft dough. Knead gently until smooth. Roll out on a floured board to a thickness of 0.5cm (¼in) and cut out circles using a 5cm (2in) cutter. Using an apple corer or a very small cutter, cut a small circle from the middle of each round and re-roll the dough to make more biscuits. Place on the prepared trays, allowing space for the biscuits to spread, and bake for 10–15 minutes until golden. Remove from the oven and leave to cool on the trays for 5 minutes before lifting on to a wire rack to cool completely. When cold, sandwich together with the jam and store in an airtight container for 1–2 days before eating.

If you don't have time to roll and cut the dough, form the mixture into balls and place on the trays. Flatten with the prongs of a fork and don't worry about making the hole in the middle.

MELTING MOMENTS

Everyone seems to have their own favourite recipe for these – sometimes made with peanuts or cornflakes, or flavoured with lemon. This one uses coconut and vanilla and is excellent accompanied by Darjeeling tea or a fragrant oolong from Taiwan or China, drunk without milk.

150g (5oz) sugar
175g (6oz) butter, softened
225g (8oz) plain flour, sifted
3 teaspoons baking powder
40g (1½oz) shredded coconut
1 teaspoon vanilla essence
10 glacé cherries, halved

Makes 20 biscuits

Preheat the oven to 160°C, 325°F, gas mark 3. Grease two baking trays. Beat together the sugar and butter until light and fluffy. Add the flour, baking powder, coconut and vanilla essence and mix thoroughly. Form the mixture into balls weighing approximately 25g (1oz) each and place on the prepared trays, leaving plenty of room for the biscuits to spread. Flatten with the palm of the hand and place a half cherry in the middle of each. Bake for 15–20 minutes until golden. Remove from the oven and leave to cool on the trays for 5 minutes before lifting on to a wire rack to cool completely.

GYPSY CREAMS

Some people define a Gypsy Cream as a chocolate or orange version of the Custard Cream, but traditionally the recipe does not include either of those additional flavourings. The soft texture and creamy filling calls for a cup of Earl Grey with its citrus notes of bergamot, or a jasmine green from China.

FOR THE BISCUITS
175g (6oz) butter, softened
50g (2oz) white shortening
   (Trex or similar)
175g (6oz) caster sugar
2 teaspoons golden syrup
225g (8oz) plain wholemeal
   flour, sifted
1 teaspoon baking powder
1 teaspoon bicarbonate of soda

FOR THE FILLING
100g (4oz) butter, softened
50g (2oz) cream cheese
100g (4oz) icing sugar, sifted
50g (2oz) cocoa powder, sifted

Makes 24 double biscuits

Preheat the oven to 150°C, 300°F, gas mark 2. Grease two or three baking trays. Beat together the butter, white shortening and sugar until light and fluffy. Add the syrup and beat again. Add the flour, baking powder and bicarbonate of soda and mix thoroughly. On a lightly floured board, roll out and cut into rounds using a 5cm (2in) cutter. Place on the prepared trays, leaving plenty of room for the biscuits to spread, and bake for 20–25 minutes until firm and golden. Remove from the oven and lift on to a wire rack to cool. To make the filling, beat all the ingredients until light and fluffy and use to sandwich the biscuits together.

MACAROONS

Dating back to 18th-century France, macaroons are a very traditional but also very modern mixture of egg whites, ground almonds and sugar. All the smartest tea places now serve tiny double-layer macaroons in different flavours and colours including rose, pistachio, matcha green tea, violet and fig, mango, raspberry and chocolate.

2 egg whites
100g (4oz) ground almonds
200g (7oz) caster sugar
25g (1oz) granulated sugar
15g (½oz) rice flour
1 teaspoon almond essence
Whole or split blanched
   almonds to decorate

Makes 18–20 macaroons

Preheat the oven to 180°C, 350°F, gas mark 4. Cover three baking trays with sheets of rice paper or non-stick greaseproof paper. Beat the egg whites for 3–4 minutes with an electric beater. Leave to rest for 4–5 minutes, then beat again until thick and white. Fold in the remaining ingredients apart from the almonds and place the mixture in a piping bag fitted with a plain 1cm (½in) nozzle. Pipe small circles of the mixture on to the paper, leaving room for the macaroons to spread. Place a whole or split almond in the middle of each and bake for 10–15 minutes until pale golden. Remove from the oven and leave to cool on the trays. If using rice paper, cut round each macaroon. If using non-stick greaseproof paper, the macaroons should lift off easily.

WHOLEMEAL SHORTBREAD

Shortbreads date back to Roman times, when the soft, buttery cake was shared by a bride and groom at their wedding ceremony to mark the beginning of a successful marriage. In later times, it evolved into a crumbly cake that was broken over the heads of the newly united couple as they stepped over the threshold of their new home to bring wealth, health and happiness.

150g (5oz) plain wholemeal flour
150g (5oz) plain white flour, sifted
150g (5oz) ground semolina
150g (5oz) demerara sugar
275g (10oz) slightly salted butter, softened
A little demerara sugar for sprinkling on top

Makes 16 fingers

Preheat the oven to 150°C, 300°F, gas mark 2. Grease an 18 x 28cm (7 x 11in) Swiss roll tin.

Mix together the dry ingredients. Cut the butter into small pieces and rub into the flour with your fingertips. Work the mixture together to form a soft dough. Press into the prepared tin, smooth the top and prick all over with a fork. Bake for 1 hour 20 minutes until pale golden. Remove from the oven and sprinkle the demerara sugar over the top. Leave to cool in the tin for about 10 minutes. Using a sharp knife, cut into fingers and leave in the tin to finish cooling.

DATE AND CINNAMON SHORTBREAD

The recipe for this spicy, fruity, indulgent shortbread comes from the Vyne, a 16th-century house in Hampshire with a working kitchen garden, the produce of which features on the menu of the restaurant. There is also a pretty tea garden.

350g (12oz) plain flour, sifted
1½ teaspoons ground cinnamon
250g (9oz) butter, softened
175g (6oz) light soft brown
    sugar
175g (6oz) stoned dates,
    chopped small

Makes 16 fingers

Preheat the oven to 180°C, 350°F, gas mark 4. Grease a 18 x 28cm (7 x 11in) Swiss roll tin. Mix together the flour and cinnamon and rub in the butter. Add the sugar and dates and stir well. Turn into the prepared tin and press down, smoothing the top with a palette knife. Bake for 30 minutes until golden. Remove from the oven and leave to cool in the tin. When cold, cut into even-sized fingers and lift carefully from the tin.

GRASMERE GINGERBREAD

Grasmere Gingerbread is rather different from other gingerbreads. Instead of being a moist soft cake or a crunchy biscuit, it is almost like a shortbread and is crumbly and light. In the 19th century, it was given as a reward to the children who brought rushes to cover the unpaved floor of the local church of St Oswald.

275g (10oz) plain flour, sifted
1 teaspoon ground ginger
½ teaspoon ground cinnamon
Pinch of salt
100g (4oz) stoned dates, chopped
150g (5oz) black treacle
75g (3oz) butter
100g (4oz) dark soft brown sugar
1 egg, beaten
¾ teaspoon bicarbonate of soda dissolved in 3 tablespoons milk

Makes 16 pieces

Preheat the oven to 170°C, 325°F, gas mark 3. Grease and line a 25cm (10in) square tin. Mix together the flour, ginger, cinnamon and salt. Add the dates. Melt the treacle, butter and sugar together over a gentle heat, then leave to cool for a few minutes. Add the flour mixture and mix thoroughly. Add the beaten egg, bicarbonate of soda and milk and blend well to a fairly wet consistency, adding a little more milk if too dry. Turn into the prepared tin and bake for 1½ hours until a skewer comes out clean. Remove from the oven and turn out on to a wire rack to cool. When cold, cut into pieces.

EASTER BISCUITS

A little like shortbread, Easter biscuits are a West Country traditional speciality. It is said that bakers in the past added the bitter herb tansy to represent Christ's suffering on the cross, and this is sometimes replicated with lemon peel today. These are light biscuits with a subtle spice and brandy flavour and a delicious crunchy topping.

FOR THE BISCUITS
175g (6oz) plain flour, sifted
50g (2oz) rice flour
1 teaspoon mixed spice
100g (4oz) butter, softened
100g (4oz) caster sugar
2 egg yolks
75g (3oz) currants
1 tablespoon brandy
½ tablespoon milk

FOR THE TOPPING
2 egg whites, lightly beaten
2 tablespoons caster sugar

Makes 10 biscuits

Preheat the oven to 180°C, 350°F, gas mark 4. Grease two baking trays. Mix together the flour, rice flour and mixed spice. Beat together the butter and sugar until light and fluffy. Beat in the egg yolks, one at a time. Add the currants, flour mixture, brandy and milk and mix to a stiff dough. Turn on to a lightly floured board and knead gently until smooth. Roll out to a thickness of 0.5cm (¼in) and cut into rounds using a 10cm (4in) fluted cutter. Place on the prepared trays and brush with plenty of beaten egg white. Sprinkle with caster sugar and bake for 15–20 minutes until crisp and pale golden. Remove from the oven and leave to cool on the trays for 5 minutes before lifting carefully on to a wire rack to cool completely.

Right: Easter Biscuits.

PEANUT AND ORANGE COOKIES

These crunchy little biscuits that combine peanuts, orange rind, syrup and oats are lovely with Ceylon tea. Ceylon has a bright, brisk flavour that is particularly suited to fruit and nut flavours and makes an excellent accompaniment to favourite teatime foods. Ceylon has been producing tea since the 1870s, when tea plants replaced the coffee bushes, which failed due to the 'coffee rust' fungus.

100g (4oz) butter
75g (3oz) light soft brown sugar
25g (1oz) golden syrup
1 tablespoon crunchy
  peanut butter
100g (4oz) self-raising flour,
  sifted
50g (2oz) rolled oats
Grated rind of 1 orange
25g (1oz) salted peanuts,
  chopped

Makes approximately
18 cookies

Preheat the oven to 160°C, 325°F, gas mark 3. Grease two baking trays. Put the butter, sugar, syrup and peanut butter into a small pan and heat gently until melted. Mix together the flour, oats and orange rind and make a well in the centre. Pour in the melted ingredients and mix thoroughly. Form dessertspoonfuls of the mixture into balls and place on the prepared trays, leaving sufficient room for the biscuits to spread. Press flat with the palm of your hand and sprinkle the tops with the chopped peanuts. Bake for 15–20 minutes until pale golden. Remove from the oven and leave to cool on the trays for a few minutes before lifting carefully on to a wire rack to cool completely.

Left: Peanut and Orange Cookies.

ORANGE CRISPS

Oranges came originally from China and are thought to have been cultivated there since around 2500 BC. By the 12th century AD, they had found their way to southern Europe and in 1493, Christopher Columbus carried the seeds from the Canary Islands to North America. The citrus tang of the juice and zest makes these little biscuits irresistible.

100g (5oz) butter, softened
150g (5oz) caster or
   granulated sugar
1 egg yolk
225g (8oz) plain flour, sifted
2 teaspoons baking powder
Grated rind and juice of
   half a small orange
1 egg white, beaten
100g (4oz) caster sugar
   for dusting

Makes approximately
24 biscuits

Preheat the oven to 190°C, 375°F, gas mark 5. Grease two or three baking trays. Beat together the butter and sugar until light and fluffy. Add the egg yolk, flour, baking powder and orange rind and juice. Mix thoroughly to a stiff paste and knead until smooth. On a lightly floured board, roll out to a thickness of 0.5cm (¼in) and cut into rounds using a 6cm (2½in) cutter. Place on the prepared trays, leaving room for the biscuits to spread, brush the top of each with beaten egg white, dust with caster sugar and bake for 10 minutes until pale golden. Remove from the oven and leave to cool for 5 minutes on the trays before lifting on to a wire rack to cool completely.

These biscuits are also excellent made with lemon juice and rind instead of orange.

APRICOT ALMOND SHORTCAKE

A delicious combination of almonds and apricots, this goes well with a golden Ceylon tea. Ceylon tea is often marketed as Orange Pekoe, which causes confusion as the name has nothing to do with orange flavouring or the colour of the leaves. It originated when the Dutch started importing tea to Europe and it was so expensive that only the Royal family – the house of Orange – and other wealthy aristocrats could afford to buy it, so the royal name became associated with tea.

225g (8oz) butter, softened
450g (1lb) self-raising flour, sifted
225g (8oz) caster sugar
2 eggs, beaten
2 teaspoons lemon juice
275g (10oz) ready-to-use dried
    apricots, roughly chopped
1 egg white, lightly beaten
50g (2oz) flaked almonds

Makes 1 x 23cm (9in)
round cake

Preheat the oven to 160°C, 325°F, gas mark 3. Grease a 23cm (9in) loose-bottomed round shallow flan tin. Rub the butter into the flour and stir in the sugar. Add the eggs and lemon juice and mix to a firm dough. Divide into two portions. On a piece of clingfilm, roll out half the dough to make a circle to fit the prepared tin. Invert so that the dough rests in the tin, remove the clingfilm and press the dough down into the tin so that it lines the base and sides. Spread the chopped apricots over the dough. On a piece of clingfilm, roll out the remaining half of the dough to make a circle to fit the top and invert on to the apricots. Press the edges well together, brush the top with the beaten egg white and sprinkle with the flaked almonds. Bake for 45 minutes to 1 hour until golden. Remove from the oven and leave to cool in the tin. When cold, remove from the tin and cut into suitable portions.

FRUITED BUNS, SCONES AND OTHER TREATS

Many of our traditional fruited buns such as tea cakes, Chelsea Buns and Bath Buns started life centuries ago as plainer breads that were enriched for festive occasions such as Easter, Christmas, New Year and saints days by adding expensive spices, dried fruits, butter and sugar to basic doughs. Today, the wonderful variety of textures and flavours offered by all these easy recipes are perfect with an afternoon cup of tea.

HOT CROSS BUNS

Although this Easter recipe is from Trerice in Cornwall, the spiced buns are, of course, traditional throughout Britain. Among the spices used is nutmeg which, during Elizabethan times, was believed to ward off plague and was therefore so valuable that a few nutmeg could be sold for enough money to set you up financially for the rest of your life.

FOR THE BUNS

25g (1oz) fresh yeast (to
    substitute dried yeast,
    see page 85)
50g (2oz) caster sugar
400ml (15fl oz) milk and water,
    mixed and warmed
50g (2oz) butter, softened
675g (1½lb) strong plain white
    flour, sifted
Pinch of salt
225g (8oz) mixed dried fruit
100g (4oz) mixed candied peel
2 teaspoons mixed spice
2 teaspoons grated nutmeg

FOR THE TOPPING

1 tablespoon caster sugar
1 tablespoon cold water
Thick paste made with 75g (3oz)
    plain flour and 3 tablespoons
    water (or trimmings from
    short pastry)

Cream the yeast with the sugar and add 150ml (5fl oz) of the milk and water mixture. Stir well, then leave in a warm place for 20–30 minutes until frothy. Grease three baking trays. Rub the butter into the flour and add the salt, mixed dried fruit, peel, mixed spice and nutmeg. When the yeast mixture is frothy, add to the dry ingredients with the remaining milk and water. Mix to a stiff dough and knead on a floured board until smooth. Form the dough into 75g (3oz) balls and place on the prepared trays. Leave in a warm place for about 30 minutes until almost doubled in size. Meanwhile preheat the oven to 220°C, 425°F, gas mark 7. Mix together the caster sugar and water for the topping. Make the stiff paste with the flour and water and roll out on a floured board. Cut narrow strips ready to make the crosses for the tops of the buns. When the buns have risen, carefully brush the tops with sugar and water and place a cross on each. Bake for 15 minutes until nicely browned. Remove from the oven and lift on to a wire rack to cool. Serve warm with butter.

CHELSEA BUNS

London's Chelsea Buns were originally made and sold in the Old Chelsea Bun House, a bakery owned and run in Pimlico, London, by Richard Hand, who was known by most people as Captain Bun.

225g (8oz) strong plain white flour, sifted

15g (½oz) fresh yeast (to substitute dried yeast, see page 85)

1 teaspoon caster sugar

125ml (4fl oz) warm milk

15g (½oz) lard, softened

Pinch of salt

1 egg, beaten

50g (2oz) butter, melted

50g (2oz) raisins

50g (2oz) currants

50g (2oz) sultanas

25g (1oz) mixed candied peel

50g (2oz) light soft brown sugar

Honey to glaze

Makes 9 buns

Grease a 18cm (7in) square tin. Put 50g (2oz) of the flour into a bowl and add the yeast, caster sugar and milk. Mix to a smooth batter and leave in a warm place for 20 minutes until frothy. Rub the lard into the remaining flour. Add the salt, the yeast mixture and the beaten egg, and mix to a soft dough. Knead on a floured board for about 5 minutes until really smooth. Place in a bowl, cover with a clean, damp cloth and leave in a warm place for 1–1½ hours until doubled in size. Knead again on a floured board and then roll out to a rectangle approximately 23 x 30cm (9 x 12in). Brush the melted butter over the surface and sprinkle the dried fruit, peel and sugar over the top, leaving a narrow border all the way round the edge. Roll up like a Swiss roll, starting with the longer side. Brush the edges of the dough with water and seal carefully. Cut the roll into nine pieces and place the rolls, cut side uppermost, in the prepared tin. Leave in a warm place for a further 30 minutes until well risen. Meanwhile heat the oven to 190°C, 375°F, gas mark 5. When the buns are risen, bake for 30–35 minutes until golden. Remove from the oven, turn out on to a wire rack and, while still warm, brush the tops with honey. To serve, pull apart and eat warm or cold.

BATH BUNS

In the 18th century, these local treats were flavoured with sherry, rose-water and caraway seeds. The more modern version uses candied citrus peel and currants and is topped with the characteristic crushed lump sugar which gives the buns their distinctive crunchy quality.

25g (1oz) fresh yeast
  (to substitute dried yeast,
  see page 85)
100g (4oz) caster sugar
550g (1lb 4oz) strong plain
  white flour, sifted
150ml (5fl oz) milk, warmed
Pinch of salt
175g (6oz) currants and sultanas,
  mixed
50g (2oz) mixed candied peel
50g (2oz) butter, melted
2 eggs, beaten
50g (2oz) lump sugar,
  coarsely crushed

Makes 20 buns

In a medium-sized bowl, cream the yeast with 1 teaspoon of the sugar. Add 100g (4oz) of the flour and the warmed milk and mix to a thick batter. Leave in a warm place for 15–20 minutes until frothy. Mix together the remaining flour and the salt. Add the remaining caster sugar, currants, sultanas and peel. Add to the yeast mixture with the melted butter and most of the beaten egg (reserving a little for glazing) and mix to a soft dough. Knead on a floured board for 2–3 minutes until smooth. Place in a lightly floured bowl, cover with a damp cloth and leave in a warm place to rise for 1½–1¾ hours until doubled in size. Grease two baking trays. Knock back the dough and form into bun shapes, each weighing approximately 65g (2½oz). Place well apart on the prepared trays, cover with oiled clingfilm and leave to rise for about 30 minutes until doubled in size. Meanwhile heat the oven to 190°C, 375°F, gas mark 5. Glaze the buns with the remaining beaten egg and sprinkle with the crushed sugar. Bake for 15 minutes until well risen and golden. Remove from the oven and lift on to a wire rack to cool.

Right: Bath Buns.
Next page: Chelsea Buns.

GINGER AND TREACLE SCONES

From Wimpole Hall in Cambridgeshire comes this spicy, richly dark scone recipe. To ensure a regular supply of quality loose-leaf tea during the years of rationing that followed World War II, the Bambridge family who lived at Wimpole Hall entrusted its entire stock of tea coupons to Twinings tea company. From 1950 to 1953 further orders for Indian tea were placed with Twinings and the tea usually arrived in 14lb cases or sometimes in 5lb packets.

225g (8oz) self-raising flour, sifted
1½ teaspoons baking powder
2 teaspoons ground ginger
50g (2oz) butter, softened and cut into small pieces
6 tablespoons milk
1 rounded tablespoon black treacle
A little milk to glaze

Makes 11 scones

Preheat the oven to 220°C, 425°F, gas mark 7. Grease a baking tray. Mix together the flour, baking powder and ginger and rub in the butter until the mixture resembles breadcrumbs. Warm the milk and treacle together in a small pan until lukewarm. Add to the mixture and mix with a round-bladed knife to a soft dough. On a lightly floured board, knead until smooth, then roll out to a thickness of 1.5cm (¾in). Cut into rounds using a 5cm (2in) cutter and place on the prepared tray. Brush the tops with a little milk. Bake just above the centre of the oven for 10–15 minutes until well risen and golden brown. Remove from the oven and lift on to a wire rack to cool. Serve warm or cold with butter.

Left: Ginger and Treacle Scones.
Previous page: Cherry and Almond Scones.

CHERRY AND ALMOND SCONES

From Rufford Old Hall in Lancashire comes the recipe for scones subtly flavoured with a hint of almonds. Although it was built in the early 15th century, long before the English learnt about tea, the house has many interesting tea-related items including various unusual teapots and a large ornate 'teapoy'. Intended to double as a small tea table and as a box that contained the tea, its name does not derive from 'tea' but from Hindi tipai, *meaning three-footed, since its sturdy leg usually ended in three carved feet.*

450g (1lb) self-raising flour, sifted
½ teaspoon baking powder
100g (4oz) butter, softened
75g (3oz) caster sugar
175g (6oz) glacé cherries,
　　roughly chopped
1 egg, beaten
A few drops of almond essence
175–200ml (6–7fl oz) milk

Makes 20 scones

Preheat the oven to 180°C, 350°F, gas mark 4. Grease two baking trays. Mix together the flour and baking powder and rub in the butter. Add the sugar, cherries, beaten egg, almond essence and enough milk to give a soft but not sticky dough. Knead lightly until smooth. On a floured board, roll out to a thickness of 1cm (½in) and cut out rounds using a 5cm (2in) cutter. Place on the prepared trays and bake for 20–25 minutes until well risen, firm and golden. Remove from the oven and lift on to a wire rack to cool. Serve with butter or clotted cream and jam.

SUE'S AMAZING ROCK CAKES

A rough sort of scone, this recipe comes from Claremont Landscape Garden in Surrey, one of England's finest gardens to be designed to blend with its surrounding natural landscape. Laid out around a lake, it has open glades and dense woodland, shaded serpentine pathways, a turf amphitheatre and a pavilion which may well have been the setting for 18th-century tea parties. Follies, grottos and temples were strategically placed to provide a peaceful venue where tea was served after the main meal of the day.

225g (8oz) plain wholewheat flour, sifted
100g (4oz) plain white flour, sifted
4 teaspoons baking powder
1 teaspoon mixed spice
1 teaspoon grated nutmeg
175g (6oz) butter, softened
75g (3oz) light soft brown sugar
175g (6oz) mixed dried fruit
1 egg, beaten
A little milk for mixing
Caster sugar for dusting

Makes 12 cakes

Preheat the oven to 220°C, 425°F, gas mark 7. Grease a large baking tray. Mix together both types of flour, the baking powder and spices. Rub in the butter, then stir in the sugar and dried fruit. Add the beaten egg and enough milk to mix to a stiff dough. Spoon on to the prepared tray and bake for 15–20 minutes until golden. Remove from the oven and dust with caster sugar. Serve warm with butter.

PEMBROKESHIRE BUNS

The recipe for these traditional Welsh fruited buns is very similar to that for Hot Cross Buns (see page 54), leftovers of which were believed to have magical powers to protect against disease and to frighten away witches and demons. Pembrokeshire Buns were made for New Year celebrations and children would go from door to door wishing everyone a happy new year, each receiving a bun as a reward.

15g (½oz) lard, softened
15g (½oz) butter, softened
450g (1lb) plain flour, sifted
50g (2oz) caster sugar
50g (2oz) currants
25g (1oz) mixed candied peel
25g (1oz) fresh yeast (to
    substitute dried yeast,
    see page 85)
250ml (9fl oz) warm milk and
    water, mixed

Makes 11 buns

Grease two baking trays. Rub the fat into the flour. Add the sugar, currants and peel and stir well. Dissolve the yeast in the milk and water and add to the dry ingredients. Mix to a soft dough and leave in a warm place to rise for 15 minutes. On a lightly floured board, knead the dough and then divide it into eleven 75g (3oz) pieces. Roll by hand to form round buns, place on the prepared trays and leave in a warm place for 10 minutes until well risen. Meanwhile preheat the oven to 200°C, 400°F, gas mark 6. When the buns are well risen, bake for 15–20 minutes until golden. Remove from the oven and lift on to a wire rack to cool.

FAT RASCALS

These fruity buns, with their rich brown crusts, are said to come originally from the Cleveland area between County Durham and Yorkshire. Thought to date back to the mid-19th century, they go especially well with a good strong cup of Yorkshire tea.

225g (8oz) plain flour, sifted
Pinch of salt
100g (4oz) butter, softened
40g (1½oz) caster sugar
50g (2oz) currants
50–75ml (2–3fl oz) milk and
    water, mixed
Caster sugar for dusting

Makes 7–8 buns

Preheat the oven to 200°C, 400°F, gas mark 6. Grease a baking tray. Mix together the flour and salt and rub in the butter. Add the sugar and currants and mix. Add enough milk and water to give a firm dough. On a floured board, roll out to a thickness of 1cm (½in) and cut out circles using a 7.5cm (3in) cutter. Place on the prepared tray, sprinkle lightly with caster sugar and bake for 20–25 minutes until pale golden. Remove from the oven and lift carefully on to a wire rack to cool.

SCARBOROUGH MUFFINS

Muffins have been a favourite since Victorian times. They were once the food of the servants who worked 'below stairs' in large Victorian mansions and the original recipes involved a mixture of leftover bread scraps and potatoes fried on a griddle. Gradually, they made their way upstairs on to breakfast and tea tables in smart dining and drawing rooms and 'muffin men' would hawk them in the street. Each region has its own recipe and this one makes a light, soft sponge that is excellent with cheese or preserves.

400g (14oz) plain flour, sifted
Pinch of salt
300ml (10fl oz) milk
15g (½oz) fresh yeast (to
    substitute dried yeast,
    see page 85)
1 egg

Makes 10 muffins

Grease two baking trays. Mix together the flour and salt. Warm the milk and stir into the yeast. Beat the egg and add to the milk. Pour into the flour and blend well to give a soft dough. Knead lightly. On a floured board, roll out to a thickness of 1cm (½in) and cut into round cakes with a 7.5cm (3in) cutter. Place on the prepared trays and leave in a warm place for 1 hour until well risen. Meanwhile, heat the oven to 200°C, 400°F, gas mark 6. When the muffins are well risen, bake for 10 minutes until golden. Remove from the oven and serve hot or warm with butter.

FRUIT SCONES

The recipe for these scones comes from Little Moreton Hall in Cheshire, a timber-framed moated manor house which was built in the late 16th century, about 100 years before the first tea arrived in England.

450g (1lb) self-raising flour, sifted
Pinch of salt
½ teaspoon baking powder
100g (4oz) butter, softened
1½ tablespoons caster sugar
1½ tablespoons sultanas
Just under 300ml (10fl oz) milk

Makes 14–16 scones

Preheat the oven to 220°C, 425°F, gas mark 7. Grease two baking trays. Mix together the flour, salt and baking powder and rub in the butter. Add the sugar and sultanas and mix with enough milk to give a soft dough. On a floured board, roll out to a thickness of 1.5cm (¾in) and cut into rounds using a 6cm (2½in) cutter. Place on the prepared trays and bake for 13–15 minutes until golden and firm. Remove from the oven and lift on to a wire rack to cool. Serve warm or cold with butter or cream and jam.

WHOLEMEAL FRUIT SCONES

This slightly less naughty – but just as delicious – scone recipe uses wholemeal flour. It comes from Killerton in Devon, where there are two tea rooms to sample, one in the house and the other with open-air seating.

450g (1lb) strong plain
    wholemeal flour, sifted
1 tablespoon baking powder
90g (3½oz) butter
50g (2oz) white Flora
a pinch of salt
½ teaspoon ground cinnamon
½ teaspoon grated nutmeg
50g (2oz) mixed dried fruit
    (such as currants, raisins
    and peel)
75g (3oz) sultanas
50g (2oz) light soft brown sugar
2 eggs
100–150ml (4–5fl oz) milk

Makes approximately
20–22 scones

Preheat the oven to 220°C, 425°F, gas mark 7. Grease two baking trays. Mix together the flour and baking powder and rub in the fats so that the mixture resembles fine breadcrumbs. Add the salt, spices, dried fruit and sugar and stir well. Beat the eggs. Add to the dry ingredients and mix with enough of the milk to give a soft dough. On a lightly floured board, pat out to a thickness of 1.5cm (¾in) and cut into rounds using a 6cm (2½in) cutter. Place on the prepared trays and bake for 15 minutes until golden brown and firm. Remove from the oven and lift on to a wire rack to cool.

EGGLESS SCONES

The name for scones seems to descend from Dutch schoonbrot *or German* sconbrot, *meaning 'fine bread', and they seem to have become part of afternoon-tea menus in the latter half of the 19th century. Despite containing no eggs, this recipe makes light, well-risen scones – perfect served warm with jam and Cornish clotted cream.*

50g (2oz) butter, softened
50g (2oz) lard, softened
350g (12oz) self-raising flour,
   sifted
100–115ml (4–4½fl oz) milk

Makes approximately
12 scones

Preheat the oven to 190°C, 375°F, gas mark 5. Grease two baking trays. Rub the fats into the flour, working as quickly and lightly as possible with cold hands. Add enough milk to give a soft, bread-like dough. On a floured board, roll out to a thickness of 1.5cm (¾in) and cut into rounds with a 6cm (2½in) cutter. Place on the prepared trays and bake for 15–20 minutes until lightly golden and well risen. Remove from the oven and lift on to a wire rack to cool.

IRISH HONEY SCONES

Should clotted cream go on the scone before or after the jam? The answer depends on where the scone is being eaten. In Devon they say that cream goes first because it is possible to get more cream to stay on the scone! In Cornwall, the cream follows the jam.

100g (4oz) plain wholemeal flour
100g (4oz) plain white flour,
    sifted
2 teaspoons baking powder
Pinch of salt
75g (3oz) butter, softened
1 tablespoon light soft
    brown sugar
2 tablespoons clear honey
50–75ml (2–3fl oz) milk

Makes 1 x 18cm (7in) round,
divided into 8 wedges

Preheat the oven to 200°C, 400°F, gas mark 6. Grease a baking tray. Mix together both types of flour, the baking powder and salt and rub in the butter. Add the sugar and mix. Mix the honey with the milk and stir until the honey has dissolved. Reserve a little for glazing and add the rest to the flour. Mix to a soft dough. Place the dough on the prepared tray and shape by hand into a flat round approximately 18cm (7in) in diameter. Divide the top into eight wedges. Bake for 15–20 minutes. Remove from the oven, glaze the top with the remaining honey and milk mixture and return to the oven for a further 5–10 minutes until golden. Remove from the oven and serve warm with butter.

WELSH CHEESE AND HERB SCONES

Obviously not intended to be eaten with clotted cream, savoury scones make a satisfying part of high tea. This recipe comes from Penrhyn Castle in Wales, which inexplicably has a Russian samovar on display. When a samovar is used, tea is brewed very strong in a small teapot which then sits on top of the central chimney until required. Half a cup of tea is then poured and topped up with hot water from the body of the samovar.

450g (1lb) self-raising flour, sifted
1 teaspoon salt
100g (4oz) butter, softened
1 teaspoon mixed dried herbs
225g (8oz) Cheddar or other
    strong cheese, grated
8 tablespoons milk
8 tablespoons water

Makes approximately
12 scones

Preheat the oven to 220°C, 425°F, gas mark 7. Grease a baking tray. Mix together the flour and salt and rub in the butter. Add the herbs and 175g (6oz) of the cheese. Add the milk and water and mix to a soft dough. On a floured board, roll out to a thickness of 2.5cm (1in) and cut into rounds using a 6cm (2½in) cutter. Place on the prepared tray, top each scone with a little of the remaining grated cheese and bake for 10 minutes until golden. Remove from the oven and lift on to a wire rack to cool slightly. Serve warm or cold with butter.

STIFFKEY CAKES

This recipe comes from Norfolk's Blickling Hall, whose kitchen often has two sugar cones on display. Sugar was always purchased in solid cones of different sizes and had to be chopped into smaller pieces with wrought-iron choppers and tongs. When tea arrived in England in the late 1650s, it was advertised and drunk as a medicinal herb and, since herbal tonics had always been sweetened with molasses, honey or sugar, tea was drunk in the same way.

350g (12oz) plain flour, sifted
1 teaspoon baking powder
25g (1oz) butter, softened
25g (1oz) caster sugar
2 eggs, beaten
A few drops of lemon essence
　　or the juice of half a lemon
Caster sugar for dusting

Makes 8 cakes

Preheat the oven to 200°C, 400°F, gas mark 6. Grease a baking tray. Mix together the flour and baking powder and rub in the fat. Add the sugar and mix well. Add the beaten eggs and lemon essence or juice and mix to a soft dough. On a floured board, roll out to a thickness of 2.5cm (1in) and cut into rounds using a 6cm (2½in) cutter. Place on the prepared tray and bake for 15 minutes until pale golden. Remove from the oven and lift carefully on to a wire rack to cool. Sprinkle lightly with caster sugar before serving.

These cakes are rather like scones and were made in the 1860s by a local woman in Norfolk called Peggy Muns. Stiffkey on the north Norfolk coast is also famous for its dark shelled cockles, known locally as Stewkey Blues.

SUFFOLK CAKES

These light buttery cakes are perfect with a cup of tea at any time of the day. When pairing different teas to different foods, choose lighter teas to suit lighter foods and stronger, more robust teas to drink with strong flavours such as beef, cheese, rich creamy cakes and chocolate. With fish, Japanese, Thai and Chinese foods, drink a green tea. White teas and oolongs are often so wonderfully light and aromatic, they are best drunk alone.

2 eggs, separated
100g (4oz) caster sugar
Grated rind of half a lemon
50g (2oz) butter, softened
50g (2oz) plain flour, sifted

Makes 10 small cakes

Preheat the oven to 200°C, 400°F, gas mark 6. Place paper cases in ten patty tins. Beat the egg whites until very stiff. Beat the egg yolks and add to the whites with the sugar, lemon rind and butter. Beat well. Fold in the flour and spoon the mixture into the paper cases. Bake for 10–15 minutes until pale golden and firm. Remove from the oven and lift on to a wire rack to cool.

SALLY LUNNS

Some say that these soft, slightly sweet cakes are named after the girl who sold them in the streets of Bath in the 18th century. Others suggest that the name derives from the French soleil lune because the tops of the Sally Lunns are golden like the sun and the base is pale like the moon. It is customary to split the freshly baked, warm cakes and fill them with cream and jam, but they make an excellent alternative to bread for favourite savoury sandwich fillings.

25g (1oz) fresh yeast (to
   substitute dried yeast,
   see page 85)
2 teaspoons caster sugar
2 eggs, beaten
300ml (10fl oz) double cream
450g (1lb) plain flour, sifted
Pinch of salt
Warm water for mixing

Makes 1 large flat cake or
5–6 small round cakes

Cream together the yeast and sugar and mix with the beaten eggs and cream. Mix together the flour and salt. Add the yeast mixture and mix with enough warm water to give a light dough. Leave in the bowl in a warm place for 1½ hours until doubled in size. Grease a baking tray. Turn the dough on to a floured board and knead lightly. Shape into one large flat cake or five or six small ones and place on the tray. Leave in a warm place for a further 20–30 minutes until well risen. Meanwhile heat the oven to 200°C, 400°F, gas mark 6. When the cakes are well risen, bake for 20–25 minutes until golden. Remove from the oven, tear open and spread with thick cream or butter. Put back together and serve immediately.

SWEETMINCE SQUARES

Filled with a sort of mincemeat mixture, this Irish recipe includes cinnamon and ginger. Under the rule of the Portuguese and then the Dutch, the island of Sri Lanka was once the world's main producer of cinnamon. Ginger has all sorts of health benefits. It can help ease nausea, reduce inflammation, settle the digestion, and minimise pain from arthritis. Both spices are also commonly used as additional flavourings for tea, added to the tea after it has been manufactured.

675g (1½lb) rich shortcrust
   pastry (see page 90)
1½ teaspoons cornflour
½ teaspoon custard powder
175ml (6fl oz) water
175g (6oz) currants and raisins
50g (2oz) mixed candied peel
75g (3oz) caster, granulated or
   demerara sugar
1 teaspoon ground cinnamon
1 teaspoon mixed spice
½ teaspoon ground ginger
A little water or milk
Caster sugar for dusting

Makes 15 squares

Make the pastry according to the instructions on page 90 and chill for at least 15 minutes. Preheat the oven to 180°C, 350°F, gas mark 4. Grease a 18 x 28cm (7 x 11in) Swiss roll tin. On a floured board, roll out half the pastry and use to line the prepared tin. Mix together the cornflour and custard powder with the water and put with all the other ingredients for the filling into a pan. Bring to the boil and simmer until thick. Turn into the pastry case and spread evenly. Roll out the remaining pastry and lay on top. Wet the edges of the pastry with a little water or milk and press well together. Bake for 45–50 minutes until golden. Remove from the oven and dust with caster sugar. Allow to cool in the tin. When cold, cut into squares.

APRICOT SESAME SLICE

As well as adding their distinctive flavour and aroma to foods, sesame seeds are rich in minerals and vitamins and also have antioxidant properties. They marry very well with the apricots in this recipe.

FOR THE BASE
100g (4oz) butter
100g (4oz) golden syrup
100g (4oz) demerara sugar
225g (8oz) porridge oats
100g (4oz) shredded coconut
50g (2oz) sesame seeds,
    untoasted
3 teaspoons ground cinnamon
Pinch of salt
100g (4oz) dried apricots,
    roughly chopped
100g (4oz) chocolate chips
    (milk or plain)

FOR THE TOPPING
25g (1oz) sesame seeds,
    untoasted

Makes 12 slices

Preheat the oven to 150°C, 300°F, gas mark 2. Grease a 20 x 28cm (8 x 11in) tin. Melt the butter and syrup together in a large pan. Add the sugar, oats, coconut, sesame seeds, cinnamon, salt and apricots and stir well, making sure that all the ingredients are evenly distributed. Stir in the chocolate chips and mix thoroughly. Turn into the prepared tin and press well down. Smooth the top and sprinkle with the 25g (1oz) sesame seeds. Press well into the mixture and bake for 30–35 minutes until golden and firm. Remove from the oven and leave to cool in the tin. When cold, cut into slices or squares.

Right: Apricot Sesame Slice.
Next page: Sweetmince Squares.

WELSH CAKES

The most famous of traditional cakes from Wales, these little flat spicy griddle cakes were offered to visitors calling at the house. Welsh cakes were traditionally cooked on a bakestone that sat on the open kitchen fire. Their name in Welsh is pice ary maen, *which literally means 'cakes on the stone'. Two variations are cooked today – Llech Cymreig is made with plain flour to give a flatter, crisper cake, and Jam Split is made by cutting the Welsh cake across the middle and filling it with jam.*

225g (8oz) self-raising flour, sifted
Pinch of salt
50g (2oz) lard, softened
50g (2oz) butter, softened
75g (3oz) granulated sugar
25g (1oz) currants
½ egg, beaten
1½ tablespoons milk
Caster sugar for sprinkling

Makes 10–12 cakes

Preheat a griddle or a heavy frying pan to a moderate, even temperature. Mix together the flour and salt and rub in the fat. Add the sugar and currants and mix with the egg and milk to a soft dough. On a floured board, roll out to a thickness of 0.5–1cm (¼–½in) and cut out rounds using a 7.5cm (3in) cutter. Place on the griddle and cook both sides until light golden. Lift on to a wire rack to cool and sprinkle with caster sugar before serving.

Left: Welsh Cakes.
Previous page: Flapjack.

FLAPJACK

Oats were always considered to be an inferior food that was often fed to horses. In his dictionary, Samuel Johnson described oats as 'a grain, which in England is generally given to horses, but in Scotland supports the people'. Today we recognize the health benefits of including fibre (good for our heart) and protein in our diet.

100g (4oz) butter
6 tablespoons golden syrup
75g (3oz) light brown sugar
225g (8oz) rolled oats

Makes 12 pieces

Preheat the oven to 160°C, 325°F, gas mark 3. Grease a shallow 18cm (7in) square tin. In a medium-sized pan, melt the butter and syrup over a low heat. Remove from the heat and add the oats and light brown sugar. Mix thoroughly so that all the ingredients are evenly distributed. Turn into the prepared tin, press down and smooth the top with a palette knife. Bake for 30–40 minutes until golden. Remove from the oven and leave to cool in the tin for 5–10 minutes, then cut into pieces and lift carefully on to a wire rack to finish cooling.

CORNISH SPLITS

Eaten as an alternative to scones, the recipe for these splits comes from Lanhydrock, originally built in the 17th century but partly destroyed by fire and rebuilt in the 19th century. Cooks and maids in its vast kitchens would have busied themselves regularly making bread, splits, cakes and biscuits to satisfy the family's teatime requirements. In the morning room each day, a table is covered with a lace cloth and set ready for tea with French china cups and saucers, silver knives and teaspoons and linen napkins.

50g (2oz) fresh yeast (to
   substitute dried yeast,
   see page 85)
40g (1½oz) caster sugar
Just under 600ml (1 pint)
   warm milk and water mixed
900g (2lb) strong plain
   white flour, sifted
1 egg, beaten

Makes 12 splits

Grease two baking trays. Mix together the yeast, sugar and warm milk and water. Leave in a warm place for about 20–30 minutes until frothy. Add the liquid to the flour with the beaten egg and mix to a soft dough. Knead until smooth and elastic. Leave in a warm place for about an hour until doubled in size. Knock back, knead again and divide into 75g (3oz) pieces. Mould by hand into neat bun shapes, place on the prepared trays and leave in a warm place for about 20 minutes until well risen. Meanwhile heat the oven to 160°C, 325°F, gas mark 3. When the splits are well risen, bake for 20–25 minutes until they just start to turn brown. Remove from the oven and cool on a wire rack. To serve, split and fill with jam and clotted cream and dust the tops with icing sugar.

MINCEMEAT CAKE

Mincemeat really was once minced meat mixed up with spices, dried fruit, lemon peel, grated apple and brandy or rum. In most modern mincemeats, the only remaining part of the meat is suet, although vegetarian varieties replace this with butter. If eating a strongly spiced cake or pastry like this at teatime, choose a tea like China black Keemun or Yunnan, a Nilgiri from southern India or a strong English Breakfast blend.

225g (8oz) self-raising flour, sifted
150g (5oz) butter, softened
150g (5oz) light or dark soft brown sugar
75g (3oz) sultanas
450g (1lb) mincemeat
2 eggs, beaten
25–50g (1–2oz) flaked almonds

Makes 1 x 20cm (8in) round cake

Preheat the oven to 160°C, 325°F, gas mark 3. Grease and line a 20cm (8in) round tin. Keeping aside the flaked almonds, put all the ingredients into a bowl and mix thoroughly. Turn into the prepared tin and sprinkle the flaked almonds over the top. Bake for 1¾ hours until a skewer comes out clean. Remove from the oven and leave in the tin for about 15 minutes before turning out on to a wire rack to cool completely.

ECCLES CAKES

Over the centuries, several regions of Britain developed their own versions of this fruit-filled pastry. Oxfordshire's Banbury Cakes are famous while, in Coventry, God Cakes were triangular to represent the Holy Trinity. Eccles cakes are thought to be descendants of cakes and loaves made as an offering at pagan and early Christian festivals.

225–275g (8–10oz) flaky pastry
   (see page 89)
25g (1oz) butter, softened
25g (1oz) light soft brown sugar
25g (1oz) mixed candied peel
75g (3oz) currants
1 teaspoon mixed spice
A little milk or water
1 egg white, beaten
2 tablespoons caster sugar

Makes 12 cakes

Make the pastry according to the instructions on page 89 and chill for at least 1 hour. Grease two baking trays. On a floured board, roll out the pastry to a thickness of approximately 0.5cm (¼in) and cut out circles using a 10cm (4in) cutter (a cup or bowl will do very nicely if you do not have a big enough cutter). Mix together the butter and brown sugar, add the candied peel, currants and spice and mix well. Place a teaspoonful of the mixture on each pastry circle. Dampen the edges of the pastry with a little milk or water, gather the edges together and seal well. Turn the cakes over so that the joins are underneath. Roll each one out so that the currants just show through the pastry and place on the prepared trays. Chill for 10–15 minutes. Meanwhile heat the oven to 230°C, 450°F, gas mark 8. Make two or three slits on the top of each cake, brush with beaten egg white and sprinkle with caster sugar. Bake for 10–15 minutes until crisp and golden. Remove the cakes from the oven and lift carefully on to a wire rack to cool.

PETWORTH PUDDING

This recipe was found in the archives of Petworth House in Sussex, although it cannot be very old as the ingredients include digestive biscuits, which only date back to the 1920s. As this has all the richness of dark chocolate, choose a strong Kenyan or China Yunnan tea to drink with it. Contains raw egg.

100g (4oz) butter
100g (4oz) granulated or
   caster sugar
25g (1oz) cocoa powder, sifted
1 egg
225g (8oz) digestive biscuits,
   crushed
50g (2oz) raisins or sultanas
50g (2oz) dark chocolate
50g (2oz) walnuts, chopped, or
   50g (2oz) shredded coconut
50g (2oz) glacé cherries,
   roughly chopped

Makes 16 fingers

Grease an 18 x 28cm (7 x 11in) Swiss roll tin. Melt the butter and sugar in a medium-sized pan. Beat in the cocoa powder and the egg. Stir in the crushed biscuits and raisins or sultanas and turn into the prepared tin. Press down well and smooth the top with a palette knife. Melt the chocolate and pour over the top. Mix together the walnuts or coconut and cherries and sprinkle over the chocolate. Place the tin in the refrigerator and leave to set. When cold, cut into fingers.

DATE AND OAT SLICES

Teatime menus today often include cakes that offer a slightly healthier option and are not so high in calories. We do now believe that tea helps to reduce cholesterol and keep our arteries functioning properly, so a cup of tea with a slice of this cake is a good teatime choice.

225g (8oz) dates, roughly
    chopped
75g (3oz) shredded coconut
75g (3oz) porridge oats
75g (3oz) plain wholemeal flour,
    sifted
40g (1½oz) light soft brown
    sugar
¾ teaspoon baking powder
175g (6oz) butter, softened
Demerara sugar for sprinkling

Makes 15 squares

Preheat the oven to 180°C, 350°F, gas mark 4. Grease an 18 x 28cm (7 x 11in) Swiss roll tin. Cover the dates with water and simmer until soft. Mix together the dry ingredients and rub in the butter to form a crumbly mixture. Sprinkle half the mixture into the prepared tin and press down lightly. Spread the softened dates over the base and add the remaining crumbly mixture. Spread evenly, press down lightly and sprinkle liberally with demerara sugar. Bake for 25–30 minutes until browned. Remove from the oven, leave to cool in the tin and then cut into squares.

DATE AND APPLE SLICES

This rich mixture of fresh and dried fruits and nuts comes from Buckland Abbey in Devon. Crunchy, locally grown apples are mixed with dates that in Britain's past were imported from such far away places as North Africa and Arabia. The long, pointed leaves are traditionally used in Christian Palm Sunday celebrations and as part of the traditional rituals on the Jewish holiday of Sukkot (Feast of the Tabernacles).

450g (1lb) Coxes eating apples, with the peel left on, cored and diced

75g (3oz) mixed unsalted nuts, roughly chopped

100g (4oz) stoned dates, roughly chopped

100g (4oz) self-raising flour, sifted

100g (4oz) dark soft brown or demerara sugar

1 tablespoon clear honey

25g (1oz) butter, melted

1 egg, beaten

Pinch of salt

Makes 10–12 slices

Preheat the oven to 200°C, 400°F, gas mark 6. Grease an 18 x 28cm (7 x 11in) Swiss roll tin. Mix all the ingredients together and beat with a wooden spoon to ensure that they are evenly distributed. Turn into the prepared tin and press flat. Bake for 30 minutes until firm and golden. Remove from the oven and leave to cool in the tin. When cold, cut into slices and lift carefully from the tin.

GINGER FLAPJACK

In North America, the name 'flapjack' applies to a pancake, but in the UK it evolved to become the name for a flat, oaty confectionery. Usually made with oats rather than flour, flapjacks are a good option for anyone who cannot eat wheat.

FOR THE FLAPJACK
175g (6oz) butter
25g (1oz) golden syrup
100g (4oz) light soft brown
  sugar
225g (8oz) porridge oats
50g (2oz) shredded coconut
1 teaspoon ground ginger

FOR THE TOPPING
175–225g (6–8oz) icing sugar,
  sifted
1 teaspoon ground ginger
1–2 tablespoons cold water

Makes 10–12 pieces

Preheat the oven to 180°C, 350°F, gas mark 4. Grease an 18 x 28cm (7 x 11in) Swiss roll tin. Melt together the butter, syrup and sugar. Stir in the oats, coconut and ginger and mix well. Turn into the prepared tin and bake for 20 minutes until golden and firm. Remove from the oven and leave to cool in the tin. When cold, prepare the topping by mixing together the icing sugar, ginger and water. Spread the icing over the flapjack and leave to set. Cut into pieces and lift carefully from the tin.

SINGIN' HINNY

The north-east of England has retained many of its traditional recipes and this is a favourite larded dough that hisses or sings as the fat sizzles during the baking. It is one of those scrummy foods that we all know is bad for us, but occasionally we need to indulge in to relive the past!

350g (12oz) self-raising flour, sifted
1 teaspoon baking powder
50g (2oz) ground rice
1 teaspoon salt
50g (2oz) butter, softened
50g (2oz) caster sugar
75g (3oz) currants
150ml (5fl oz) double cream
150ml (5fl oz) milk

Makes 1 x 23cm (9in)
round cake

Preheat a griddle or a large, heavy frying pan to an even, moderate temperature. Mix together the flour, baking powder, ground rice and salt and rub in the butter until the mixture resembles fine breadcrumbs. Add the sugar and currants and mix well. Add the cream and milk and mix to a stiff dough. Knead lightly until smooth. On a lightly floured board, roll out to a circle 23cm (9in) in diameter and about 0.5cm (¼in) in thickness. Place on the griddle or pan and cook for 4–5 minutes on each side until golden. Serve hot or cold, cut into wedges and spread with butter and jam.

IRISH POTATO CAKES

Irish recipes make inventive use of potatoes and working people relied heavily on recipes that mixed them with milk, buttermilk, cream and eggs to make breads and cakes and these traditional savouries. Other traditional potato specialities include dippity, *a mixture of raw grated potatoes, flour, milk, eggs and salt cooked in little round cakes,* champ, *made with mashed potatoes, spring onions, milk and butter, and* boxty, *a mixture of potatoes cooked as pancakes, dumplings or bread.*

100g (4oz) cold mashed
  potatoes
100g (4oz) plain white flour,
  sifted
50g (2oz) lard or dripping
Pinch of salt
A little milk

Makes 6 cakes

Preheat the oven to 200°C, 400°F, gas mark 6. Grease a baking tray. Mix together the potatoes and flour and rub in the fat. Add the salt and enough milk to give a soft, pliable dough. Roll out on a floured board to a thickness of 1cm (½in) and cut into rounds using a 6cm (2½in) cutter. Place on the prepared tray and bake for 15–20 minutes until golden. Remove from the oven and serve piping hot, spread lavishly with butter.

These traditional savoury cakes are excellent served for breakfast, tea or supper.

SUCCESSFUL BAKING

INGREDIENTS

FLOUR

- **Plain flour** is generally used when little rise is required; for example, in pastries and shortbreads. To convert plain flour to self-raising flour, add baking powder in the quantities recommended on the container for different types of baking.
- **Self-raising flour** is used for cakes that need a raising agent. In some recipes, however, the amount of raising agent already added to the flour may be too great, so a mixture of plain and self-raising flour is used.
- Always store flour in a cool, dry place, preferably in an airtight container. Sift to remove any lumps and also to incorporate extra air before adding to the cake mixture.

RAISING AGENTS

- **Baking powder** is the most commonly used raising agent. It gives off carbon dioxide, which forms bubbles in the mixture. These expand during cooking, making the cake, scone or biscuit rise and helping to produce a light texture. Too much baking powder can cause sogginess and heaviness.
- **Bicarbonate of soda** is often used in recipes that include sour milk or buttermilk, spices, treacle and honey.
- **Sour milk** is sometimes necessary to give extra rise to heavy

mixtures, such as gingerbreads. It can be made at home by allowing milk to sit in a warm atmosphere until it curdles.

- **Buttermilk** is a standard ingredient in Welsh and Irish cookery and can be found in some supermarkets and from some milk-delivery companies.
- **Yeast** was once the only raising agent available for home baking, but is now generally used only in bread-making and in some traditional fruit or spice breads or pastries, such as saffron loaves, Chelsea buns and lardy cake. Dried yeast keeps for several months in an airtight container. Fresh yeast lasts for about a week in the refrigerator and will freeze for up to six months. Fresh yeast is often available from large supermarkets with bakeries, or local bakers. You may have to ask for it as it is not a 'shelf' item, but it is frequently free of charge.

Dried or instant yeast can be substituted for fresh yeast. For 15g (½oz) fresh yeast use 6.25g (¼oz) dried or instant yeast, for 25g (1oz) fresh yeast use 10.5g (½oz) dried or instant yeast and for 50g (2oz) fresh yeast use 21g (¾oz) dried or instant yeast. If using dried yeast, dissolve in a little liquid of the recipe before adding to the other ingredients. If using instant yeast, add to the dry ingredients before mixing in the other ingredients. If using dried or instant yeast, the dough only needs to rise once.

FATS

- **Butter** and margarine are interchangeable in most recipes, but butter is preferable in shortbreads and rich fruit cakes, such as Christmas cake, that are to be stored for some time and matured before eating.
- **Lard** is often used in biscuits and gives a shorter texture.
- **Oil** is excellent in carrot cakes and chocolate cakes, and is ideal for anybody with a cholesterol problem.

- Allow butter, margarine or lard to soften to room temperature for at least an hour before using. Soft or whipped margarines can be used straight from the refrigerator.

EGGS

- Eggs should be at room temperature, as they are more likely to curdle if taken straight from the refrigerator.
- Small eggs (sizes 5 and 6) are too small for most recipes. Use large (sizes 1 and 2) or medium (sizes 3 and 4).

SUGAR AND OTHER SWEETENERS

- **Caster sugar** is generally used for creamed mixtures as it gives a much lighter texture than other types.
- **Granulated sugar** is acceptable in rubbed-in mixtures, but can produce a slightly gritty texture. It is worth paying a little extra for caster sugar.
- **Demerara sugar** is good in tea breads and in mixtures where ingredients are melted together, such as gingerbreads and boiled fruit cakes. It is excellent for sprinkling on the top of loaves and biscuits.
- **Soft brown sugar** gives a caramel flavour and beats well in creamed mixtures. The darker variety has a stronger flavour.
- **Black treacle** has a dark colour and strong flavour and is often used in gingerbreads and some fruit cakes.
- **Golden syrup** gives a soft, moist, sometimes sticky texture which is suitable for gingerbreads and flapjacks.
- **Honey** adds a very special distinctive flavour but too much will cause the mixture to burn easily.

PREPARING TINS

Most non-stick cake tins are very reliable if you follow the manufacturers' instructions but, to be on the safe side, it is wise to line and grease them anyway. Grease tins with whatever fat or oil is to be used in the recipe, then line with non-stick greaseproof parchment. Cut a single piece for the bottom of the tin and, when fitting paper to the sides, cut into the corners to make quite sure that it lies neatly against the tin. It may also be necessary to cut and overlap the paper, as the sides of circular tins sometimes slope slightly.

OVEN TEMPERATURES

Always make sure that the oven has reached the correct temperature before putting in the item to be baked. If you are not sure whether your oven is accurate, buy an oven thermometer and make regular checks. If using a convection oven, reduce all recommended temperatures by 20°C (68°F).

CAKES, SCONES AND BISCUITS

Always use the right tin for the recipe. Smaller or larger tins will affect the cooking time and hence the texture of the finished cake or biscuits.

Except in fan-assisted ovens, most cakes and biscuits cook best in the middle of the oven. Rich fruit cakes, large cakes and shortbreads should be placed just below the centre, and small, plain cakes, Swiss rolls and scones just above.

Do not disturb the cake during the first three-quarters of the baking time or, better still, not until you think it may be ready. Draughts and knocks can make the cake sink.

When placing biscuits on prepared tins, always allow room for them to spread during baking. It is better to leave too much room than to have all the biscuits merging into one misshapen mass.

IS IT READY?

To see if a sponge cake is ready, press lightly with a finger; if it springs back, it is cooked. To test fruitcakes and gingerbreads, stick a skewer into the middle of the cake and withdraw it immediately. If the skewer comes out clean, the cake is done. If not, allow a further 15 minutes and test again. Biscuits are usually ready when they are just turning golden. Scones are firm, well risen and golden when cooked.

If a cake begins to darken too quickly, place a double or triple layer of greaseproof paper over the top and continue cooking as usual.

PASTRY

The aim is to make pastry as light as possible, and this depends on how much cold air is trapped in the mixture before baking. The secret is to use cold ingredients, to have cold hands, cold bowls, a cold slab or surface on which to roll (marble is ideal) and to work in a cool room. Work quickly and lightly, using the fingertips when rubbing in, as too much handling makes the pastry tough. When rolling, sprinkle only a little flour on to the work surface and use light, even movements.

Most pastry recipes call for plain flour, but self-raising is sometimes used for suet crust and shortcrust. The more fat is used, the shorter the pastry will be; if the amount of fat is less than half the amount of flour, add 1 teaspoon of baking powder for each 225g (8oz) of flour. Butter, or butter mixed with lard, is best.

Rich pastry needs a hotter oven than others. If the oven is too cool, the fat will run out of the pastry and the pastry will be tough and chewy.

LINING PIE DISHES AND PLATES

Roll out the pastry to a thickness of about 0.25–0.5cm (⅛–¼in) and a little larger in size than the prepared dish or plate. Lay the pastry carefully on the dish, making sure that no air is trapped underneath. Do not stretch the pastry as it will only shrink back. If it is not big enough, roll out a little more and try again. Ease the pastry into all the rims and corners of the dish, then trim off any surplus. (Trimmings may be useful to make crosses on Hot Cross Buns [page 54] or a trellis over the top of a tart or pie.)

BAKING BLIND

This is necessary when an uncooked filling is to be put into the pastry case, or to set the pastry before any filling is poured in and cooked. When the prepared tin has been greased and lined with the pastry, prick the base all over with a fork. Cover the base with a piece of greaseproof paper followed by a layer of metal baking beans (available in any good cookware shop) or pasta or pulses (dried haricot beans, dried kidney beans or chickpeas). Bake in a preheated oven for just under the required time, then remove from the oven, lift out the baking beans and the greaseproof paper and bake for 5 minutes more to dry out the base.

PASTRY RECIPES

FLAKY PASTRY

450g (1lb) plain flour, sifted
1 teaspoon salt
350g (12oz) butter, or half butter and half lard, softened
1 teaspoon lemon juice
300ml (10fl oz) cold water

Mix together the flour and salt. Divide the fat into four portions. Rub one portion into the flour with your fingertips. Mix in the lemon juice and cold water to give a soft dough, rather like the consistency of butter. Knead gently on a lightly floured board until smooth. Roll out to a rectangle three times longer than it is wide. Dot the second portion of fat over the top two-thirds of the surface. Fold up the bottom third and fold down the top third and seal the edges by pressing together with a rolling pin. Wrap in clingfilm or a plastic bag and chill for 15 minutes. Place the dough on the floured board with the folded edges to your right and left, and roll out again to a rectangle. Repeat the dotting, folding and chilling process twice more until all the fat is used. Wrap again and chill for at least 45 minutes before using.

450g (1lb) plain flour, sifted
1 teaspoon salt
450g (1lb) butter, softened
1 teaspoon lemon juice
75–100ml (3–4fl oz) iced water

PUFF PASTRY

Mix together the flour and salt. Add 50g (2oz) of the butter, cut into small pieces, and rub into the flour until the mixture resembles fine breadcrumbs. Add the lemon juice and enough water to give a soft dough, similar to the consistency of butter. Knead lightly until really smooth. In a clean linen cloth, shape the remaining butter into a rectangle. On a lightly floured board, roll out the pastry to a rectangle slightly wider than the rectangle of butter and about twice its length. Place the butter on one half of the pastry and fold the other half over. Press the edges together with a rolling pin. Leave in a cool place for 15 minutes to allow the butter to harden slightly. Roll out the pastry to a long strip three times its original length, but keeping the width the same. The corners should be square, the sides straight and the thickness even. The butter must not break through the dough. Fold the bottom third up and the top third down, press the edges together with a rolling pin, put inside a well-oiled plastic bag and chill for 30 minutes. Place the dough on the floured board with the folded edges to your right and left, and roll out into a long strip as before. Fold again into three and chill for a further 30 minutes. Repeat this process four times more and chill for 30 minutes before using.

This is best made over two days, rolling three times and chilling overnight before completing the rolling the following day.

450g (1lb) plain flour, sifted
A good pinch of salt
350g (12oz) butter, softened
2 egg yolks
4 teaspoons caster sugar
3–4 tablespoons cold water

RICH SHORTCRUST PASTRY

Mix together the flour and salt. Rub in the butter until the mixture resembles breadcrumbs. Make a well in the middle, add the egg yolks and sugar and mix with a round-bladed knife. Add enough of the water, a little at a time, to give a stiff but pliable dough. Knead lightly until smooth. Wrap in clingfilm or a plastic bag and chill for at least 15 minutes before using.

450g (1lb) plain flour, sifted
A pinch of salt
350g (12oz) butter, softened
1 teaspoon lemon juice
3–4 tablespoons cold water

ROUGH PUFF PASTRY

Mix together the flour and salt. Cut the butter into small pieces and stir lightly into the flour with a round-bladed knife. Make a well in the middle, add the lemon juice and mix with enough water to give an elastic dough. On a lightly floured board, roll out the dough to a long strip, keeping the sides straight and the corners square. Fold up the bottom third and fold down the top third and turn the dough so that the folded edges are to your right and left. Repeat the rolling and folding process three times more, chilling the pastry for 15 minutes between the third and fourth rolling. Chill for at least 15 minutes before using.

450g (1lb) plain flour, sifted
A pinch of salt
100g (4oz) butter, softened
100g (4oz) lard, softened
3–4 tablespoons cold water

SHORTCRUST PASTRY

Mix together the flour and salt. Cut the fats into small pieces and rub into the flour until the mixture resembles fine breadcrumbs. Gradually add enough water, mixing with a fork, to give a stiff, but pliable dough. Knead lightly for a few minutes until smooth. Wrap in clingfilm or a plastic bag and chill for at least 15 minutes before using.

BREAD

FLOURS

The most commonly used flour for breadmaking is wheat. Strong wheat flour has a high gluten content and gives a better volume of bread, as it absorbs more water and makes a lighter dough. **White flour** is made from the starchy part of the grain from which the fibre and wheatgerm has been removed. **Wholewheat flour** is made from 100 per cent of the grain; nothing is added and nothing is taken away. **Wheatmeal** is made from 81–85 per cent of the grain and some of the fibre and wheatgerm has been removed.

Bread can be made with various other grains. **Rye** gives a dark dough and is usually mixed half and half with wheat flour; **barley** gives a cake-like texture and is usually mixed with wheat flour; **maize** gives a crumbly, crunchy texture. Other ingredients can be added to achieve different results: for example, extra bran, wheatgerm, sesame, poppy or sunflower seeds, cheese, herbs, spices, lemon or orange rind and rye flakes.

KNEADING

Kneading is an essential part of breadmaking as it helps to develop the gluten and the rise of the dough. Flour a board and use the palms of your hands, almost to the wrists, to push and turn the dough. As you work you can actually feel the texture changing to a smooth, elastic but not sticky consistency.

PROVING

Always cover the dough when setting it to prove; any draughts may affect the process. The yeast in the dough needs warmth to start working; the ideal temperature is between 36 and 44°C (98 and 110°F). Too much heat will kill the yeast; too little will stop it from working. The best place to leave dough to prove is on top of an Aga, a boiler or an active tumble dryer. The time taken for the dough to rise will depend on the warmth, but it usually takes 1–1½ hours. The second rising is quicker, usually between 20 minutes and half an hour.

BAKING SOLUTIONS

FRUIT CAKES

- If the fruit sinks to the bottom of the cake, it is probably because there was too little beating of fat and sugar, too much liquid or too much raising agent.
- If the cake sinks in the middle, it may be because the oven was not hot enough, or there was too little creaming of fat and sugar, or there was too much raising agent.

- If the cake is dry, it is usually because there was not enough liquid, or it is overcooked.
- If the top of the cake is cracked, the tin was too small and the oven was too hot.

SANDWICH AND SPONGE CAKES
- If the outside is too dark and the inside is not properly cooked, the oven was too hot and the cake was too near the top.
- If the top of the cake is domed, the oven was too hot or there was not enough beating.
- If the sponge does not rise well, there was either too little raising agent or the oven was too cool.

SCONES
- If the scones are tough, there was probably too much kneading.
- If the scones are hard and not spongy, there was too little liquid.
- If the scones are soggy in the middle, the oven was too cool or they were too low in the oven.
- If the scones have not risen, there was too little raising agent.

YEASTED BREADS AND CAKES
- If the loaf or cake is smaller than expected, there was either too much or too little raising agent, or the yeast did not activate properly due to incorrect temperature during proving.
- If the texture of the loaf or cake is coarse, the yeast was not properly mixed at the beginning, or there was too much yeast, which caused excessive rising and air in the dough.

INDEX

Irish Potato Cakes 83
puff pastry 90

Raisin and Bran Bread 21
rich shortcrust pastry 90
Ripon Christmas Bread 28
Rock Cakes, Sue's Amazing
59
Rolls, Sesame 18
rough puff pastry 91
Rufford Old Hall 58

Saffron Cake 27
Sally Lunns 70
Scarborough Muffins 62
scones
    Cherry and Almond
        Scones 57
    Eggless Scones 65
    Fruit Scones 63
    Ginger and Treacle Scones
        57
    Welsh Cheese and Herb
        Scones 67
    Wholemeal Fruit Scones
        64
sesame seeds
    Apricot Sesame Slice 72
    Sesame Rolls 18

shortbread
    Date and Cinnamon
        Shortbread 46
    Wholemeal Shortbread 45
Shortcake, Apricot Almond
    51
shortcrust pastry 91
Singin' Hinny 82
Soda Bread, Bateman's 15
Standen 21
Stiffkey Cakes 68
Sue's Amazing Rock Cakes
    59
Suffolk Cakes 40
Suffolk Fourses 33
Sweet Wholemeal Bannock
    25
Sweetmince Squares 71

tea breads
    Bara Brith 32
    Barm Brack 31
    Blackberry Tea Bread 29
    Date and Walnut Loaf 23
    Derbyshire Spiced Easter
        Fruit Bread 22
    Honey Tea Bread 37
    Orange Tea Bread 30
    Saffron Cake 27

Sweet Wholemeal Bannock
    25
treacle
    Ginger and Treacle Scones
        57
Trelissick 29
Trerice 54

walnuts
    Date and Walnut Loaf 23
Welsh Cakes 73
Welsh Cheese and Herb
    Scones 67
Wholemeal Fruit Scones 64
Wholemeal Shortbread 45
Wholewheat Bread 22
Wimpole Hall 57

yeast 85